COLORFUL

Leadership™

How Women of Color Transform Our World

Gloria S. Chan, JD, PCC

CoachDiversity Press

Copyright © Gloria S. Chan

To my sister, Silvia

Table Of Contents

Acknowledgements..2

One: Women of Color, Feminine Alchemists of Our Time 4

Two: The Awakening: The Journey from Self 1.0 to 2.0...................................16

Three: Our Foundation: Unconditional Self-Love 21

Four: Healing the Parent-Child Relationship....................................... 23

Five: Stepping Into Power Through the I.M.P.A.C.T. Principle™ 36

Six: I. is for Inspiration & Intuition... 37

Seven: M. is for Mindset 62

Eight: P. is for Passion & Purpose...103

Nine: A. is for Alignment 121

Ten: C. is for Courage 145

Eleven: T. is for Transformative Leadership 164

Twelve: The Personal Is Global: The Journey from Self 2.0 to 3.0..............185

Thirteen: The Power of Shadow Work...187

Fourteen: Our Shadows and Systemic Change.................................. 191

Fifteen: Grieving the Race Card 197

Sixteen: A Lifetime Worthy of YOU..204

Using This Book as a Study Guide..207

Seeking Guidance?...208

About the Author.. 210

ACKNOWLEDGEMENTS

Dear Lord, thank You for using me, for writing through me, for always guiding me, for never leaving me.

Thank you Mom and Dad for always supporting me and believing in my vision. To Daniel, Conrad James 志聰, and Cassiopeia, you are the lights of my life, and we are always together. Silvia, this book is for you. John and Rini, thanks for loving my sister. Dr. Towanna Freeman, thank you for your vision, for your trust in me to be a part of it, and for our powerful sisterhood. Elisha P. Brown, this writing would not be possible without your help. Thank you for loving my son.

To all the women of color from whom I have learned so much: First Lady Michelle Obama, The Honorable Patsy Mink, The Honorable Judy Chu, The Honorable Mazie Hirono, The Honorable Tammy Duckworth, The Honorable Grace Meng, The Honorable Doris Ling-Cohan, May Chen, Karen Narasaki, Irene Hirano, bell hooks, Yuri Kochiyama, Grace Lee Boggs, Beyoncé, Rosie Abriam, Maria Meier, Ann Kalayil, Mee Moua, Bel Leong-Hong, Francey Youngberg, Kathy Ko Chin, Doua Thor, Tina Matsuoka, Lisa Hasegawa, Deepa Iyer, Linda Akutagawa, Christine Chen, Vida Benavides, Martha Watanabe, Dr. DJ Aida, Susan Jin Davis, Miriam

Yeung, Theresa Mah, Allison Brown, Kimberly Thomas Rapp, Sarah Ha, Christy Brown, Hayya Lee, Sandra Paredes, Lizet Ocampo, Lucienne Canet, LiYun Alvarado, Lillie Madali, Darnyelle Jervey, Jamie Borromeo, Tuyet Duong, and Jenny Yang.

To those who took a chance on me and countless other young leaders: mentors The Honorable Michael M. Honda, The Honorable Norman Y. Mineta, Jennifer Van der Heide, Gary Simons, and Laurie Meadoff; youth and educational institutions: Prep for Prep, CityKids Foundation, The Spence School, Swarthmore College, Harvard Law School; to the neighborhoods that shaped my identity and values: to Starrett City, to East New York, to Douglaston Queens, to NYC's Chinatown, to the Upper East Side. To the Jewish momma mentors who cared for all of us students of color: Mary Frosch, Professor Cynthia Halpern, Dean Martha Minow. To the youth of Chinatown Youth Initiatives. To the present and future community of *CoachDiversity Institute*™.

To Jeren Hope, who first taught me about big faith. To Danilo Rivera, and all of my god-siblings. To my Prep family. To my dear friends Renée Mayo, Haegi Kwon, Elizabeth Lee, and Delonte Gholston.

To my brilliant editors: Dana Chapnick and LeaNora Ruffin. Thank you!

ONE

....

WHY I WRITE:
Women of Color, Feminine Alchemists of Our Time

I am a woman of color.

Most people, when they look at me, would not see a woman of color.

As an Asian American woman, I know that it may be strange to some for me to declare so prominently that I am a woman of color. My experiences after all are very different than those of African American women or Latina or Native women. I know that I am positioned differently and have unique privileges as a fair-skinned woman. We all have unique perspectives and experiences. But, here is what's connects us: we have all interfaced with systems of racial injustice in a world where racial healing is sorely needed. We have been raised in communities and spaces where we have witnessed so much pain and trauma from these systems.

Here is our choice: *We get to thrive anyway.*

Colorful Leadership™ is a step-by-step guide to leading and living life in Full Color. It is inspired by women of color, written by a woman of color, and written for women of color. It is about connecting to personal power, agency, and choice, in environments that may not always recognize our uniqueness, our genius, and our talents.

When I think about who I am, I know from the depths of my soul that I am a powerful being. I am truly uncontained and unlimited by any social box or category. I am beyond labels.

Yet, in this moment in time, my purpose is intimately connected with being a woman of color.

My parents are immigrants from China. For the first 10 years of my life, my family and I lived in a housing complex in Brooklyn called Starrett City. Starrett was deep into East New York, so deep that we were on the water, between a landfill and John F. Kennedy airport. At the time, it was also one of the largest, highly subsidized housing complexes in all of New York City, established with the intent to provide racially integrated housing.

Starrett became famous for a 1988 lawsuit in which its racial quota system was challenged and prohibited. Today, Starrett is still studied by urban planning and policy students as a case study of racial integration.

Needless to say, I grew up in an incredibly diverse neighborhood, surrounded by immigrants from all around the world: Asians, Africans, Latinos, and Russians. Many Black and White Americans resided in Starrett too. So, from the beginning, I have been acutely aware that I am one among many people of color.

Sometimes when people hear where I am from, they say, "wow, you're from the projects!" or "you're from the 'hood." The truth is, growing up, I didn't know what "the 'hood" meant and truly didn't have any judgment around it. I was oblivious to the drug paraphernalia at the playground, and thought the violent Halloween chaos that caused my elementary school to close early to get little ones home safely was par for the course. I viewed my community as a wonderful, tree-lined, family-oriented place, complete with a swimming pool and everything! My parents even had a supportive social network of Chinese immigrant families at the apartment complex.

When I was 9, my parents entered me into a program that took minority academic achievers out of public schools and into the most elite private schools in the entire world. We became the early racial and economic diversity of New York City's private schools. It was an academically rigorous program, through which I have bonded with my peers for life. My peers were predominantly African American and Latinos. Asian kids were also in the program, but we were a very, very small percentage. So again, I found myself in another incredibly diverse community.

As a teen, I grew up both on the streets with my Chinatown friends, and also in the diverse spaces of youth empowerment. I was among the first youth in New York University's Asian American leadership program that began in the mid-90s. My student leadership was all related to Asian American identity, and even in diverse spaces, I often represented the Asian American voice and perspective.

In many of these diverse spaces, I found myself once again as one of a few Asian Americans among many other racial and ethnic groups. My very first best friend was Black, and my first teen love was also Black. I grew up in a time when "Asian" was not yet hip. There weren't any Asians on television, except maybe that one Asian chick in the rap videos - but her boobs were WAY bigger than mine.

My style in the 1990s was inspired by the likes of Aaliyah, and the women of TLC. I sported hair slicked back in a bun or ponytail, with one dangling curl perfectly hot-ironed with not one strand out of place. I wore dark red lipstick with even darker lip liner. I stood 5' 1" tall and wore Tommy Hilfiger and size 38 jeans. Hip hop was the music of choice. At this young age, I was already crossing the boundaries and lines of racial and ethnic identity.

By the time I was a young adult, I was undoubtedly a person of color.

And womanhood? What of it? It's difficult to grow up in our time-space reality and not feel the impact of gender roles.

In my fresh (wo)man year at college, there was about an entire week when I just grieved being a woman. I cried unstoppable tears.

I was filled with sadness over sexism: I was sad that girls grow up in a world where they are fed Disney's fantasies of feminine weakness and the need for being saved through romantic love with a man. It didn't matter that I had a boyfriend at the time. I was still sad! I was sad that these early childhood messages were reinforced through the advertising industry, the media, and any Hollywood film or romantic comedy I saw. I was sad that in Chinese ancestral family trees, when a woman is married, she gets expelled from her own family tree and annexed to her husband's.

I mourned the brainwashing and conditioning I — and all the powerful women I knew — underwent. It was as if I didn't exist. My Korean American boyfriend at the time was confused. My roommate didn't know what was wrong with me. My therapist who was an Asian American woman also had no clue. I was so mad!!! I thought: isn't this why the school hired YOU? So you could understand students like ME? I felt completely isolated, voiceless, and invisible. I was experiencing the full array of emotions experienced in the early stages of the grieving process: sadness, anger, and loneliness.

Throughout my teens and twenties, I felt particularly lonely. I longed for love. More specifically, I wanted Asian American love. So many of my Asian American friends felt ostracized, picked on, made fun of for not being American enough. We were told to be quiet in the home, and then laughed at for being too shy or dorky out of the home. Asian sisters had no voice, and our brothers had to prove manliness to counter stereotypes of small penises and the lack of bravado or swag. If you didn't identify with your gender, well then you were stuck in no man's land and shit out of luck. I wanted Asian love to bring healing and validation in our private lives in ways that were not available in our public ones.

I wanted redemptive, real love within and among "oppressed communities." I wanted love to empower us for the sake of community. I wanted love for myself, but more importantly for those struggling around me. I wanted so badly for real Asian American love to redeem, heal, and empower us for social change in entire communities.

The versions of Asian American love and belonging I found around me failed to meet my desires. They felt empty and fake. Behind that judgment was definitely jealously. As a small-chested Asian, I didn't feel feminine enough to fit in. I was the smart, private school kid, the "little sister" hanging out with older Asians in the streets of Chinatown. The Asian American frat parties on the college scene didn't feel right either. There, all the most attractive girls were skinny, had curves, dressed in black, and wore flawless makeup. It was a standard of beauty that I felt like I couldn't and wasn't inspired to attain. My older sister, who had the chameleon-like superpower to be accepted socially no matter what the mold, had started wearing gray-colored contact lenses and smoking cigarettes in an effort to fit in and be cool. In my jealousy, I judged her behavior as lame and superficial.

In an effort to control my body, and gain attention from my Asian American male counterparts, I felt I needed to be even smaller and skinnier, and struggled with bulimia and anorexia throughout this period. At this time, I felt completely unlovable and invisible.

I longed for companionship and deep conversation. Since I didn't find anyone doing or writing about Asian American love in a way that I really wanted, I read about Black love, and became absorbed in bell hooks's trilogy on love. I cherished *This Bridge Called My Back: Writings by Radical Women of Color* by Cherrie Moraga and Gloria Anzaldua. I found my community in books filled with the longing for love, and validation from women of color writers of all stripes.

I adored the idea of romantic love and found comfort in the notion that love itself could save people of color, individually, and as entire communities. I still believe that, but love for me today means something totally different than what it meant back then. Back then, I saw our communities as filled with victims, and saw myself as an advocate for victims. I was desperate for redemptive love that would soothe the pain of victimhood, and if I didn't have it, I was not whole. I also took it upon myself to "love" on people until they were healed, and if they did not accept my "redemptive" love, I took it as a statement of my personal worth. Today, I know wholeness on new powerful levels, for myself, and I see this same powerful potential in our communities.

As my identity developed through my family, neighborhoods, school, a career in law and politics, and now as a coach, I began to integrate all of these circles of influence. I discovered I wasn't just an Asian American woman.

I am a woman of color.

Eventually, I found myself as a leader of the Asian Pacific American community in our nation's capital. It came up in conversation with another Asian American leader in DC politics that there was a perception that I was more connected with Blackness than being Asian American. I would get questions from my Asian American colleagues wondering about this. They would ask, "WHY Gloria? You are not Black!"

And I've had similar inquiries from friends and colleagues in the Black community. When I was shaping this book, I shared with an older, Black, female mentor that the book would be for women of color. She too asked me, "WHY Gloria? You are Asian! WHY?" Perhaps as a Black woman with different life experiences, she did not did not understand how I too could identify as a woman of color.

My life experience, in relation to our nation's history and systems of oppression, have led to my development as a woman of color.

So, as a woman of color, my calling today is to inspire and commune with other women of color. In this moment, we are birthing a movement. A movement of women who push boundaries and accept no limits. A movement of women who revel in *all* their gifts of receptivity, intuition, collaboration, connectedness, and oneness. A movement of women who also assert their gifts of confidence, action and manifestation. A movement of women who unabashedly embrace the full spectrum of these gifts to empower themselves and step into leadership. If these words resonate with you, then it is to you that I write.

Let us move together beyond the confines of structural norms and how we have been defined by society. Let us move forward into a space of unlimited power to discover what INSPIRES us.

Here's what inspires me.

When I look at my clientele, the women that inspire me the most, they are mostly Black women, Asian women, Latinas, and some White women too. These women are in the trenches doing social justice work to empower communities. These inspiring women are on the verge of stepping into their full power to change the world for the betterment of those still suffering in their communities.

Working with these women, my heart sparks. In this age, there is something so special and unique about the "feminine," which means different things to different people. The old ways of force, aggressiveness, domination, and dictatorship are no longer working. And mainstream thought is catching up to the fact that we need new ways of leading and new ways of being.

It is also a particular experience to be a woman from historically marginalized and oppressed communities. As a woman of color, I honor the very real ways that our communities face structural racism and discrimination, and how sexism makes deep imprints on our psyche.

Today, as we reclaim ourselves, there is nothing keeping us from reaching our full power and potential. And in that power, there are no victims.

Our experiences in these deeply entrenched systems of power have uniquely: 1) impacted the way we incorrectly view ourselves internally as disempowered or limited beings; and 2) simultaneously given us an unbridled, compelling desire to uplift and empower our communities in deep, meaningful, and sustainable ways.

We are the feminine alchemists of our time.

What do I mean by alchemy? For me, alchemy is the mysterious, subtle, magical process of transforming that which is seemingly base, ugly, and useless into something powerfully creative, redemptive, and unconditionally loving. Alchemy is the subtle process of individual transformation that has powerful and ever-expanding ripple effects throughout our relationships, communities, nations, Earth, and throughout space and time.

We are the feminine alchemists of our time.

We are doing the hard work to empower ourselves, to come home to our selves, to connect with our Higher Purpose, and allow our soul's expression. With a passion and desire for change, we transform ourselves, forgiving the pain from our pasts, to create lasting legacies.

We are the feminine alchemists of our time.

We are part of the spiraling, ever-expanding evolution of humanity. We have a powerful role to play as systems change.

We are at the intersection of it all.

As it stands, society is built upon the duality of gender, assigning clearly defined roles and characteristics to women and men. This creates rigid societal constructs without space for individuals who do not conform to these norms. My mission and calling in this season is to help create space for women of color so we are able to tap into *all* of our power. I want to help us bolster our leadership, assertiveness, confidence, action, and vision. At the same time, I am called to remind us also draw upon our powers of intuition, receptivity, empathy, and connectivity.

Once we achieve this balance and embrace *all* of our various attributes, we can step into our full power and begin to heal ourselves and our communities. Only by achieving this balance will we bring our vision into reality, and make the impact on history for which we are destined.

By empowering ourselves, we manifest our legacies, and provide healing and ultimately empowerment for our communities. Because of the pain and trauma we have faced as individuals, and that which our families and communities have faced, we have a beautiful vision of human and community potential; a world in which human potential is not limited by race or ethnicity, immigration status, gender identity, or physical or mental ability; a world that uplifts *all* of humanity, and honors freedom of the human spirit for *all* people.

Our visions are powerful, and they deserve our care and attention. They deserve to be brought into fruition.

The world needs us! Now!

Come with me. Let us honor our pain by healing it and letting go of the past.

In so doing, we can emerge powerfully and move forward with strength and purpose.

Come with me, and I will show you how to live life in Full Color, stand powerfully in your leadership, and bring your vision into full reality right here in this lifetime. You will be living the life of your dreams. And you will be the answer to the prayers of so many.

This book is for you
This is not a typical book on leadership. This book is for my 25-year-old self, the one who struggled to find her own voice in bookstores and libraries. This book is for my blood sister, and the rest of my sisters.

This book is for all the women who are ready to be firestorms.

While this book has been inspired by and written for women of color, its wisdom is universal. Through this book, I am creating the space for women of color to live life in Full Color and unleash our pure genius. In this book, I guide you step-by-step through my I.M.P.A.C.T. Principle™. You will learn to drop resistance and expectation to then connect with a powerful part of yourself, walk in true connection to Spirit, develop your big voice, step into full power, and ultimately live freely and make huge leadership impact.

The purpose of this book is to inspire boldness, get you in touch with your legacy, purpose, and ultimate freedom; help you make the impact of your lifetime, and finally discover your true power.

This book is an intimate look into how we do the hard work of unpacking shadows to transform and expand, ever-growing, ever-healing. This is a step-by-step guide for how *anyone* can do the same.

This book is an intimate look into how we continue our processes of becoming — becoming the ever more powerful version of ourselves. This book is a guide to shaking the foundations on which our identities are based, and letting go of identities that no longer serve.

This book is inspired by and written for women of color.

This book is for you.

Who you are
You have a deep yearning for something different and new. You want to live life purposefully, and you are not sure how to go about it. You may know exactly what your purpose is, but are simultaneously terrified and exhilarated to move into it. Or you may not have the slightest clue what your calling is, and yet have a deep knowing that what you're doing right now is not working.

14

This book is for you if you are stressed out, burnt out, and unfulfilled. This book is for you if you are tired of stress and conflict in relationships, work, and family life; if you are feeling like you are playing small, and leaving passion, fulfillment, peace, and even exhilaration on the table. This book is for you if you are ready to start creating a new life for yourself, and writing a different story for yourself. This book is for you if you are ready to do the hard but exhilarating work of homecoming — coming into one's own self through the practice of radical authenticity.

Whether you are just starting out in your career, the seasons are changing in your life, or you just got shocked into waking up to yourself through some life-changing event, this time of stepping into the unknown may invoke a mixed bag of emotions: fear, exhilaration, anxiety, stress, excitement, and a yearning for freedom on the other side.

I honor each of you as you take these next courageous steps. Take comfort that we are all in this together. Even if we have been around this block for a while, we continue to evolve, and we continue to feel these new areas of unchartered territory. As we continue to grow, evolve and expand, we are becoming more of who we are.

Let us start with waking up.

Two

....

THE AWAKENING:
The Journey from Self 1.0 to 2.0

You change for two reasons:
Either you learn enough
that you want to, or
you've been hurt enough
that you have to.

- Unknown

Welcome to the Awakening! This is the moment in our lives where we notice that the world around us was previously a prison of our own making, and where we begin to get a glimpse of our own true power to create a life we love. This is the moment where we create a shift in mindset: where we move from allowing fears and external expectations from family, others, and society to control us, to actively choosing our lives based on our own desires, visions, and creative instincts.

Your Awakening is a time of transition and can often be full of raw emotions. Despite these emotions, it is important to celebrate the choice you have made to enter this period of Awakening. So, if you are struggling through your Awakening, congratulations!

As the quote above says, "we change for two reasons: either we learn enough that we want to, or we've been hurt enough that we have to."

My coaching clients come to me at these precious moments of Awakening. Some may be seeking clarity in personal relationships. They might realize they finally need to step up and voice their deep concerns with their spouses and partners, and ask for the space to do the work of self-discovery. And others are seeking change in their professional life. They may have burnt out at their jobs and are ready for rest and reflection. Or they may realize they are holding back their powerful voice at work and are stressed because they are not yet asserting their leadership potential. Or still some may be creative souls who feel trapped in less-than-creative professions or positions they thought would lead to accomplishment, praise, and achievement. Regardless of the client, they all have one thing in common — they are ready to ask the tough questions of what they truly want, and are making the bold moves into a brave, new world where they are pursuing their dreams.

Many clients who seek my services are women who are passionate about social change and progress, but are coming out of dysfunctional and abusive relationships either in their personal or professional lives. These relationships may serve as self-sabotage and hold us back from fulfilling our full potential.

Such was the form of my Awakening - I had come to the point that I had been hurt enough that *I had to change*. My journey from Gloria 1.0 to Gloria 2.0 came in the shape of a difficult relationship in my late twenties with a 45-year-old multi-racial singer-songwriter. The relationship involved psychological, emotional, and physical abuse, in addition to sexual trauma.

This abusive relationship can best be described as mutualistic. Mutualistic relationships generally do not involve harmful behavior. However in this instance, we created an entanglement that was simultaneously unhealthy and addictively beneficial for all involved.

In the midst of this completely dysfunctional relationship, my bank accounts were drained, credit limits were reached, and student loans were defaulted. I was emotionally and spiritually stripped to the core and found myself completely socially isolated. My partner and I both abused alcohol and drugs. In fact, the only times he was nice to me was when we were under the influence of both. From my view and through obsessive internet research, I concluded that he likely suffered from depression, anxiety, paranoid personality disorder, and aggressive behavior. Certainly, he was an addict to drugs and alcohol, as much as I was an addict to his emotional abuse. I clearly was not loving myself unconditionally with full acceptance of who I was.

That period was a necessary wake-up call from which I have absolutely benefited. I realize the word "benefit" may cause some pause. But it's true. I benefited. It was the best thing that happened to me at that time. It was the turning point that started it all. It forced me to finally begin my quest to learn how to truly love myself. Through self-love, I was able to attract my spouse, which led to the birth of my son. It gave me the gumption to transition from one professional community to start my own business in a new field. I am ultimately so thankful and feel truly blessed! So, yes, that whole experience was a huge benefit. I couldn't have orchestrated my Awakening any other way. The Universe's master plan is always better than the one we could craft for ourselves.

Until that break-up, I didn't realize that my approach to life was suboptimal. My romantic relationships had been unsatisfying, but I always pointed the finger outward, blamed the men I dated, and didn't explore what I was doing that was leading to unfulfilling results. I didn't realize I wasn't living in Full Color. I didn't realize I was not fully aligned with my power and inner genius. I never looked inward.

The entire period from my teens through my twenties were characterized by the juxtaposition of incredible academic and professional achievement, and wholly unsatisfactory romantic pursuits. I was addicted to loveless-ness, and wasn't awake enough to be conscious of it as a problem. After all, I was fine and achieving great success in my schoolwork, extracurricu-lar leadership activities, and my career. One area of success made the oth-er area of emptiness tolerable — for a time.

I devoted countless waking hours putting energy into trying to convince myself, and the men I chose, that I was worthy of love. If a man was wholesome and loving, I became bored and moved on, and the more a man didn't want me, the more I was interested. I was addicted to the drama that accompanied these incomplete relationships. And so, God, All-That-Is, the Universe sent me this desperately needed wake-up call so I could begin to stop that recurring, unloving voice in my head.

After the abusive relationship ended, I felt relief and freedom. I felt blessed to be given a second chance at life. This was my shot at cleaning out my physical world, and cleaning up my brain and emotional world. I had made it out alive. I felt cared for. I felt like I could breathe again. It was my chance to start fresh, and finally love myself. This was the start of my spiritual journey home to my True Self.

In the face of all this heaviness, that relationship forced me to look deep within. Here, I discovered my power and inner genius. Then, and only then, was I able to make the necessary changes in my life, to move from being a victim to become fully re-aligned with my power and inner geni-us, and thus live in 100% radical authenticity. This was my Awakening.

So, if you have arrived at that crunchy, painful place, congratulations. Truly, congratulations. You are in for the ride of a lifetime. For it is not until the Awakening that we realize our own power and genius.

Throughout the book, I will also invite you to do some reflection of your own. I recommend that you find a beautiful journal that inspires you to keep track of any insights you gain about coming home to Your True Self, and beginning to live life in Full Color.

Here's to our Awakenings. It's time to wake up!

Three

....

Our Foundation:
Unconditional Self-Love

The foundation of *Colorful Leadership*™ is 100% unconditional self-love, with a radical commitment to living authentically. This is the fundamental belief that we are worthy of unconditional love. It is the realization that we are an essential part of the Great Divine. It is a return home to the soul.

Before we can possibly commit 100% to creating a life that fulfills us, we need to first believe that we are worthy of that life. Radical self-love and self-acceptance is the focus during the Awakening. In many ways, this awakening is a spiritual one.

Self-love may not happen overnight. Consistent self-love is an in-depth process of stripping away years of programming and learning to think for ourselves.

In so many ways, we dishonor and are not awake to the Divine in us. We attack our self-worth every time we are hard on ourselves or beat ourselves up for not being this way or that, for not being accomplished enough or pretty enough, for being too skinny or too fat, for being too dumb or unskilled. We beat ourselves up for not being perfect, when we are more Perfect than we know.

In order to create a life that we love and deserve, we must stop that incessantly tape of an unloving voices in our minds. Some of these messages we are aware of, and others, we are not. When we do this, we brainwash ourselves with recurring messages of unworthiness.

It is our time for radical self-love. From this foundation of unconditional love of self, we can finally become an integrated whole and start living the life of our dreams. We can finally start honoring our passion and purpose.

So how do we create spaces for self-love?

EXERCISE: In what ways are you harsh with yourself? In what ways do you beat yourself up? How ready are you to stop? How can you begin to be more gentle with yourself and care for yourself as a Divine being?

Four

....

Healing the Parent-Child Relationship

Before you find your public voice,
you have to find your private voice.

To create a strong foundation of self-love, we need to heal our relationships with our parents and become adults.

Clearing out dysfunctional and unproductive energy with our families of origin and the families that raised us is one of the single most important thresholds we cross to step into powerful leadership. Whether you are leading movements, groups, nonprofits, teams, governments, corporations, families, or even just yourself, healing this parent-child relationship will change your entire approach to life.

Whether our parents were absent or present, whether they are still around or whether they have passed on from this earthly plane, making things right with our parents, and the ability to be fully ourselves in this foundational relationship is one of the most fundamental steps we can make as we develop our *Colorful Leadership*™.

Our relationships with our parents affect the choices we make in every aspect of our lives, from our leadership decisions, communication style, our relationship with authority, our career choices, our relationship choices, how we view money, and how gently we treat others, and most importantly, how we treat ourselves.

This threshold is not just for those in their teens, twenties, or thirties. I have coached seasoned executives well into their lives who still harbor resentments and other unforgiving emotions toward their parental units. This affects their courage, faith in themselves, and their belief system.

Particularly as women of color, our relationships with our mothers, are deep and complex. We've been taught to be humble, to obey our parents, to be faithful children. In immigrant families, these relationships can be extra complex with the added layer of guilt and sacrifice that fills the narrative that flows from one generation to the next. Any disagreement with the parental generation can be interpreted as ingratitude, disobedience, and self-centeredness.

Standing in our own power takes constant conditioning and practice. This includes holding true to our own ideas, and using our voice to share and express these ideas. This also includes not overcompensating, and making room for the ideas and opinions of others. All of these may be wholly underdeveloped muscles, given our culture and our society.

For me, the most conflict-ridden relationship has been the one with my mom. I have always loved my mother, however, it hasn't always been easy to get along. My evolving relationship with her has had tremendous impact on my leadership style, confidence, and more. After all, how you condition yourself to show up in one area of your life directly affects how you show up in all others. So getting along and improving your relationship with Mom is not only about Mom, it's also about shifting the way you show up in the rest of your life too, including your career and leadership.

One way to get along with mom is my old way. What I used to do for at least two and a half decades was agree with everything she said, followed all instructions — or at least let her believe that I was following all instructions. If she believed that I was adopting her thoughts as my own, exactly how she thought them, there would be peace, and in many cases, some version of intimacy and closeness. I used to question why my sister would fight back so much and disagree about the littlest things. There would be so much yelling in the house that I would plead to my sister, "can't you just say yes and just agree with her?!"

After my Awakening, the old way didn't work for me. Always conforming to the needs and wants of a dominant figure didn't give me much practice in speaking my Truth and expressing who I truly was. And Gloria 2.0 needed the space.

For protection, I began labeling my mom as a "Tiger Mom," not to stereotype all Asian moms, but more my way of naming past patterns, and create distance. The old way gave me some deep practice in perfectionism, self-judgment, criticism, defensiveness, and failing to deeply explore my own personal values, much less honoring them — in other areas of life. I needed space from this practice to create room for new ways of being.

There are other ways to co-exist with family. My new way of loving my mother is still evolving and will continue to evolve for the rest of my life. While each journey is unique, there are key lessons that have shaped my journey over the past years.

Create the Space to be Yourself

I used to blame my mom. Traits of my emotionally abusive relationship in my late twenties seemed too eerily similar to my relationship with my mom all these years. There was no space to have my own thoughts. There was only one Truth (hers), and if I had a different interpretation or a different opinion, I was just plain wrong, immoral, a liar, a cheater, and ulti-mately, disobedient and not good. There was no space to think. There was no space to be me!

And so I needed to create space for me. After my challenging relationship, I did my deep soul-searching. I developed routines of self-care that in-cluded meditation, journaling, and support groups. I pasted loving mes-sages all over my refrigerator door. I reconnected with loving and sup-portive friends. I prayed. I healed myself and became stronger. I followed my own bliss and not anyone else's, and began to express my own opin-ions. I needed to train myself to be myself, and that was difficult around a domineering personality.

After developing stronger boundaries through fewer phone conversations with mom and fewer visits home, she began accusing me of arrogance, and equated my love for myself as being "snot-nosed."

But I stood strong. I continued to make a space for myself, unabashedly. I give you the same advice. Make space to be yourself. There is no need to defend your unconditional love for yourself to anyone else: not even a Tiger Mom. Take as much mental, emotional, physical, and spiritual space that you need. Do you need peace? Alone time? Time away from family?

For some, there is physical and emotional abuse. And in these relation-ships full of violence, aggression, manipulation, hatred, and shame, it is okay to take a lot of space, even full on separation. It is okay to cut the cord.

And get this: there's no need to feel guilty. Taking the time to discover who you are will help you build your relationship with your parents in the long run. Are they ill? At the end of the line? Take less space! Have they passed on? Take the time to love yourself now. It will help release any emotion around what type of parent you wished you had, and will help you love them even more, even as they have passed.

EXERCISE: In what ways can you create more space to be your authentic self? How can you express to yourself unconditional love? In what ways can you treat yourself and be gentle with yourself?

Trust That Things Get Better

For me, things were distant for a while, perhaps a year or two; and they needed to be. After some healing, things shifted. There was a time, after the Awakening, that I just couldn't stand my parents' typical arguments any longer.

And then one day everything came to a head. It was May 2011, after planning my first successful big gala at the Asian Pacific Institute for Congressional Studies, I went home to New York to speak at a civic engagement panel, and then visited my parents' home for the evening. After this whirlwind of gala-planning and travel, I was exhausted and in no mood for anything but peace, rest, and home. In all honesty, I wanted to be showered with praise, love, and comfort. I wanted my parents to be proud of my accomplishments. And that desire was valid and normal.

As my dad pulled into the driveway with my mom and I in the car, we started talking about home.

I was so tired and delirious that I blurted out "I just want to go home."

My dad responded, "but this is home. Your parental home should be your home."

I hadn't meant to offend him. Before I could explain, my mother jumps in and starts blaming my father for all the things that he did that made their home not "home" in my eyes. And that was the straw that broke the camel's back. How dare she use my fatigue and emotion to take jabs at my father? I was so tired of getting in the middle of their stuff that I decided that I didn't want to spend *any* time in that house, not one second, even if it was 11pm at night. I knew I would not get the experience that I really needed in that moment.

I needed peace and decompression, not more stress. I grabbed my suitcase out of the back seat, and walked briskly and decidedly down the street. I walked and I didn't turn back. This wasn't a brash moment of teenage behavior. This was an adult choice.

I called my future husband, whom I was dating at the time, and he navigated me through the streets of Douglaston, Queens, out of my parents' neighborhood, until I found my way to the Long Island Rail Road Station. It was perhaps a 30 minute walk from their house, and I when I got to the station, I finally started my peaceful 5-hour journey back to DC where I could finally rest and be myself.

It was that night, as a 30-year old woman, that I finally stood my ground, and ran away from home for the very first time.

Things gradually got better. Phone conversations got easier. Today, I don't go crazy after a phone call with my mom. Today, my internal world doesn't implode after spending a night at my parents' house. And the parents feel the change too. Not all at once, but mom notices. I am kinder and am more open. I have my own thoughts and make space for them. I don't need to express them nearly as much. Things change. Sometimes, slowly; sometimes quickly, but they do change.

EXERCISE: What is your relationship with your parental figures? How do you communicate with them, if at all? How do you feel in relationship with your parental figures?

Don't Make Your Peace of Mind and Joy Contingent Upon Your Parents' Reactions

Your parents do not have to understand everything in your heart right now. You may have different value systems from them, and different lenses through which you interpret the world. They might not agree with you or believe your perspective is valid. And that is okay. You don't have to convince them that your values and beliefs are worthy of time and space. They don't have to understand you in order for you to be happy.

Conversations with my mom used to be a lot like being in court, fighting for the validity of one position over the other. My mom often is solely focused on the need to validate her own position. This is completely normal for someone who rarely received any validation in her formative years, and who has been trained not to accept validation in her adult life. I understand that vulnerability more now, and embrace it. I am more forgiving.

Today, with respect to my own validation, I know that I only have to "win" in one "courtroom." My thoughts, emotions, and actions need not be validated or judged by anyone. They only need to be aligned with who I am in the moment, based on my values in that moment. They only need to be aligned with the impact that I want to make in this lifetime. I am under the jurisdiction of my own values and that of my higher power. And in this venue, I am always unconditionally loved and accepted.

My Happiness is Not Contingent Upon My Parents' Understanding of Who I Am

It is a primal, normal, valid desire to want understanding from our parents. In fact, it is central to our innate need to belong. However, making our happiness contingent upon their understanding gives away all of our personal power. It can de-stabilize and overwhelm. It can take the ground from beneath our feet. In fact, the old adage is awesome: what others think of me is none of my business. Difficult to apply to our own mothers? Or is it?

By a total epiphany, by complete grace, it came to me that how I enjoy my relationship with my mother need not depend on whether she understands me or whether I feel heard. Hallelujah! Freedom is here!

As her understanding of me becomes less integral to how I enjoy our relationship, she becomes more understanding of me. Amazing.

How My Parents Recall the Past and How I Recall the Past Are Equally Valid

I no longer need my mother to adopt my version of the past, and I need not adopt hers. The tortuous efforts of convincing are no longer necessary! This brings great happiness and serenity!

My mom often recalls the past. She has suffered through quite a bit of trauma during the Cultural Revolution, during her transition to the US, and her American life. It is hard for her to recall happy times. I don't recall her ever recalling a happy moment. Many of her recollections include the myriad of ways that people have wronged her. And she reminds me about it, including how she believes I abandoned her when I was 25 years old – ten years ago at the time of this writing!

I never interpreted my behavior as abandonment, and her recollection used to annoy me! I used to need to correct her record of history. As I shifted my approach and actively decided not to correct my mother's version of history, she too has shifted, and now brings up these past experiences less and less. I accept her experience. Freedom is here. Amazing.

EXERCISE: Think of common arguments that occur in the relationship between you and your parental figures. Take the time to validate all perspectives. In what ways are your own viewpoints valid? In what ways are their viewpoints equally valid? How willing are you to accept that all viewpoints are valid?

Appreciate The Gifts You Have Received From Your Parents, As YOU Define Them

Hold incredible gratitude for the gifts you have received from your parents in all forms. Hold *your own* gratitude, defined on your own terms. This gratitude is not what your parents tell you to be grateful for. This is gratitude and love for your parents on *your* own terms. There are the obvious gifts, and also the gifts that come in the form of challenges.

For me, my mom did an amazing job with what she had. Given her own childhood and challenges, like all of us, she did the very best she could. She morphed from a garment worker to a journalist and a writer. She educated herself with a B.A. and an M.A., all while raising us. Through the commitment and tenacity of my mother, I had tremendous exposure to the arts, access to the best education possible, nutritious meals, and learned to always push myself to excellence.

Many of these were privileges she never had for herself, and so she gave them to my sister and me. These are tremendous gifts. Challenges with my Tiger Mom have also been gifts. The difficulties have given me strong self-care habits, have led to my evolution as a conscious human being, and have given me tremendous empathy and compassion for those I serve today who struggle with these very issues. I credit my parents — particularly my mother — with much of my life's learning and my very capacity to love and serve. So today, I refuse to grin and bear what I feel is abusive behavior. Instead, I open my mind and heart in order to appreciate, accept and truly love the gifts my mom has given me, all of them.

EXERCISE: Express gratitude for your parental figures on your own terms. What do you truly appreciate about your upbringing? What gifts have they given to you, even if they were in the form of challenges? How has your upbringing shaped who you are today? What do you love about yourself today?

Love Your Parents the Way You Want to be Loved

Be the change you wish to see in the world. Love them how you want to be loved, with *complete* acceptance — no expectations, and no judgment. Love them from up close. Love them from afar. However it works for you, love and accept them for exactly who they are, right now, on their own journey. Love them, now, how they are right now, because everything is as it should be; because every moment is a gift to grow; because from each moment is a lesson and a calling to be more open, to love more, and to be more yourself. Today, I love my mom during her moments of beautiful clarity, her moments of self-awareness, and through her struggles, her accusations, her loud decibels — I love it all — when I remember who I truly am.

> AFFIRM:
> I choose to be my best self always,
> even around my parents.

It is not always easy to be my best self in a contentious relationship. My very best qualities include being joyful, engaged, inspired, light-hearted, and light-spirited. You wouldn't know this if you were my mother during my transition from Gloria 1.0 to 2.0. Late last year, after my son was born, she noted to me that I'm nicer to our dog Cassie than I am to her. And she was right! I was so protective and defensive around my mother that I was not my joyful self, the self that I share with Cassie.

Finally, when my son was 4-months-old, I became tired of that. I was fed up with always getting triggered and defensive around my mother. And like we discussed before, *we change for two reasons: either we learn enough that we want to, or we've been hurt enough that we have to.* I needed to change. I started by setting the intention to let go and accept. Then things started to change. I began to see my mother in a different light, to treat her better than our dog, and to love her completely. I began to be my best self. This moment has been five years in the making.

>   AFFIRM:
>   **Being my best self, I create new happy moments.**

It is in this new place of full, unconditional acceptance that I test new ways of being and creating new happy moments with my mother — and with everything else. Hallelujah.

> EXERCISE: What might unconditional love for your parental figures look like? What fights are you ready to let go of? How ready are you to accept your parental figures for who they are and love them anyway? What would make it safe for you to do that?

Drop the Labels or Make New Ones

On New Year's Eve of 2015, I decided that I would never again call my mom a "Tiger Mom." I realized that my mom is only "Tiger Mom" when I think of her as one.

How is this possible you say? Well, the truth is that we alone are the ones that assign meaning in our lives. If I believe my mother to be "Tiger Mom," I will interpret every word out of her mouth to be aggressive, judgmental, controlling, annoying, and something that I am ready to pounce on, resist against and get annoyed by or ignore or suppress. And, what we resist persists. In reality, her intentions are never to be aggressive, judgmental, controlling, annoying, etc.

There cannot be a "Tiger Mom", when there is no "Tiger Cub" to resist her. My very labeling of her as "Tiger Mom" made the peace I coveted completely impossible. As I choose to step away from the wild mental ride that is the "Tiger Cub," I am able to see her more clearly and listen to her more intently. I am able to assign her new roles, like "Holder of Wisdom That I Seek" or "Fierce Courageous Woman Warrior" or "Another Soul Seeking Itself" or "Scholar" or "Keeper of Family Stories and Secrets" or "My Lovely Hero" or "My Inspiration" or "The Amazing Woman Who Holds the Family" or "The Generous Provider." When these are the labels I choose to assign to her in my mind, a warm and humane connection is possible.

Dropping our unproductive labels leads to greater leadership, effectiveness, productivity, and inspiration.

EXERCISE: Who do you label? At home? In the workplace? In the community?

Which labels are no longer productive? Who are you ready to understand more? With whom are you ready to be more present?

In dropping these labels, where will you experience more peace and openness?

Congratulations, you've done the work to begin to heal your relationship with your parents.

Remember, this can be done whether you remain in contact with your parents or whether you are no longer in contact with them. I have met many women who are in recovery from deeply emotionally, physically, and spiritually abusive relationships with their birth mothers. And sometimes distance is needed with those relationships.

Trust that your power and confidence will continue to grow. Thing continue to get better. As you start to use your voice in private, your public voice and influence will grow stronger. As we shift into higher levels of awareness and understanding, all of our relationships shift as well.

Now, it's time to step into our power.

FIVE

....

Stepping Into Power Through the I.M.P.A.C.T. Principle™

Through this book, I will be walking you through the I.M.P.A.C.T. Principle™, upon which my own journey of self-discovery, and all my services are based. So sit back, relax, enjoy the ride, and enjoy the stories.

I am so excited that you are here.

I congratulate you, and I honor you.

Let's begin.

....

SIX

I. is for Inspiration & Intuition

Inspiration doesn't just happen.

I help amazing people create inspired lives and careers. You might read your social media feeds with disdain and annoyance, watching people sharing their joy. You may think to yourself, *"Go shove it!"* and ultimately underneath that, there may be some *"I wish I had some more of that."* Even those sharing may be putting up a front of joy, and are actually more tortured that they are projecting.

Well, I'm here to share that there's a great myth about inspired living and inspiration. The myth is that inspiration is a random light bulb that just goes off, unplanned without us doing anything. Inspiration just hits!

Ever notice that inspiration hits some people a lot more than others? Why is that? Is the Universe so unfair as to shower some with great favor, and others with nothing but despair?

The truth is that while yes, inspiration hits us like flashes of brilliance, you have to do the work to make sure your own circuitry is ready for the light bulbs, and ready for the great ideas. Inspired living is actually a daily and routine practice, and a joyful one at that!

As we get better at listening to our intuition, and get out of our own way, the flashes of insight and brilliance will happen naturally, and more often. We will become much more aware of the synchronicity around us, and notice that everything has a purpose in aiding our growth and evolution. When we focus our attention and energy on any area of our lives, it gains momentum. Before you know it, you will be a lightning rod for inspired thought and action. Things begin to happen faster and with greater ease.

However, you have to create the fertile ground for that to happen. You have to do the work to be open enough for inspiration to come, to recognize it when it does, and to follow-through with inspired action.

When rewiring your brain for inspired living, it all starts with intuition.

The Sacred Gift

The intuitive mind is a sacred gift and the rational mind is a faithful servant. We have created a society that honors the servant and has forgotten the gift.

— Albert Einstein

We all have incredible intuition to tap into. Working on our intuition means developing the capacity to listen to our own internal wisdom and guidance. It is making space to know your own Truth. It means making space to listen for the guidance that we all have from within. It means connecting with our personal power. It means letting the callings from our soul drive and power our goals in the world.

As we seek the work we love, as we search for our purpose and passion, as we strive to make the impact and leave the legacy of a lifetime, we must also get in touch with and learn to trust our own internal wisdom and guidance. We cannot bring about new visions if all we are doing is replicating what already exists by following expectations of the status quo.

If we follow the status quo, we get the status quo.

To cultivate new ideas we must begin to be guided by our own hearts, our own passions. To bring our vision into the world, we must pause long enough to listen, and to see. We must take the time to connect with our internal wisdom to bring forth what we are meant to do in our lifetimes. If we want the world to change, we must change.

While we don't know everything, there is a part of each of us that is connected to Infinite Wisdom. Intuition is hard to pin down to words because it is beyond logic and reason. It means knowing without any logical explanation. For some, it means receiving spiritual insight.

We all have gifts of insight and wisdom. Some traditions call it the connection to the Soul, or Spirit or God or G-d or Allah or All-that-Is. Others might call it the Universe. Some call it Energy or Source. You might call it your "gut feeling" or "instinct."

It doesn't matter what you call it. There is a part of you that is unseen and all-knowing. It knows what knowledge to share with you at any given moment in time. It knows what you are ready to hear. It knows how to sooth you, and assure you. It is the part of you that knows what to say to make you feel better, more confident, more sure. It pushes you beyond your fear. And there, beyond your fear, you will find your real power.

On Faith

I didn't grow up with an overt practice of faith in the home. My family did not go to church. We did not go to temple. We did not pray together. My popo - my mother's mom - attended a church in New York City's Chinatown, where she would take English classes. Each Chinese New Year, we did make offerings as a family to my grandparents who have passed on, and again during the Qing Ming festival, but that was really about it. I had a sense that my parents may have believed that the offerings were to real spirits, but we were never taught to communicate or draw strength from our ancestors as a routine practice of faith. As a kid, I remember my mother bringing me to temple one time to light some incense when things got bad, but I never saw what a regular practice of faith and spirituality looked like.

I did have healers and artists on my mother's side of the family. My gong gong, my mom's dad, was a Chinese herbal doctor. On the weekends when my sister and I would visit him at his doctor's office, he shared with us his knowledge of traditional Chinese medicine. When he was in between appointments, he also taught us qigong and kungfu, which are physical practices that also involve spiritual and mental focus. I have aunties that have followed his suit and are practicing Eastern medicine and energy healing. Another auntie practices astrology, and is a student and author of a book on Chinese medicine, quantum physics, and energy. Mindfulness was certainly something introduced in those limited hours with our gong gong, but otherwise we existed in a rather rambunctious and reactive Cantonese extended family life.

Although Eastern traditions permeated my home culturally, daily spiritual practice and mindfulness were not among those traditions growing up. Instead, our home was brimming with the financial and emotional stress the comes with a new immigrant household. By the time I was a young adult, I was unsure of how to process and sit with my emotions, and hadn't yet explored how to access spiritual insight and growth.

So how did I begin my spiritual journey? In my twenties, a friend passed along the book *Peace is Every Step* by Thich Nhat Hanh. This Vietnamese monk's accessible writing was my first introduction to mindfulness as a daily practice. In that book, he taught that no matter what situation is before you, we can find joy through the breath and present moment awareness. I used Buddhist philosophy and meditation to cope with the drama-filled relationships of my twenties. I had a brief introduction to a hatha yoga practice in the gym of the House of Representatives when I worked in the U.S. Congress.

It wasn't until the Awakening, however, that I started to truly understand my spiritual power. That's when I started to come alive.

After I left my dysfunctional relationship, I began participating in a 12-step program called Adult Children of Alcoholics And Other Dysfunctional Families. In the rooms of these meetings, my faith started to blossom. I don't have active alcoholism in my family. However, the Cultural Revolution and the immigrant experience caused enough trauma to my parents to create family dysfunctions that permeated into other relationships in my life.

At these meetings, I discovered the importance of acknowledging how this world is harsh on our souls; that we are taught to suppress who we truly are from an early age, right from the start. Having grown up in the harsh political environment of the Chinese Cultural Revolution, my parents weren't taught how to love themselves unconditionally, much less love their children this way. The world we live in, as it is, does not equip parents with full capacity for self-love, and hence self-love is not taught to the young. We are taught not to express ourselves. We are taught to meet standards in schools. We are taught perfectionism or rebellion. We are taught that we must act in certain ways to fit in, to be successful, to conform. Consequently, all of us need healing and a homecoming to the soul.

So through this 12-step program, I found my voice, my truth, and my Higher Power. I learned to listen to my inner voice and to express it for the first time in adult life. I was able to express my authentic self in ways that I couldn't in my prior relationships, in law school, or on Capitol Hill.

The way that these spaces work is that you share. You share deeply. You share in agony. You share in celebration. You share with shame. You share in fear. You share in bravery. You share as honestly as you feel comfortable. You share in safety. What you share is heard and accepted with no questions asked, no comments given, no advice offered. We are just given the space to be. And the more honest we get, the more we are transformed. So, I got honest. And the more I was honest, the more I transformed.

To live a powerful life in Full Color, we must have big faith. That faith may take many forms. It could be faith in our compassion, humanity, and human progress. It could be faith in the learning and growth process. It could be faith in evolution. It could be faith in a higher power, God, Allah, G-d, Spirit, Universe, ancestors, deities, guides, or angels.

No matter what you believe, it is important to believe. And here's why. We only receive as much as our faith will allow.

Repeat, *we only receive as much as our faith will allow.*

If we believe we are worthy of only small things, we feel small, and con-sequently, we only pursue and receive small things. But, if we believe we are an essential, unique part of a big, beautiful, and limitless divine fabric; that all of us are essential, deserving, beautiful, and whole; and that all of us are connected; then we can believe anything is possible — for us and for others. We believe that we are all as well-meaning as we can be in the moment, we are all are doing our very best, and we are all deserving of a life in Full Color.

EXERCISE: Journal about your faith.

- Describe your faith. Where do you draw your faith? What sustains you? Where do you draw emotional and spiritual support? When do you always feel safe? What do you believe in? A Higher Power? Ancestors? Spirit guides? A way of living? Humanity? Community? Family? Yourself? Your potential?

- In what ways can you regularly draw upon your faith? How do you stay connected to your faith? When do you feel most powerfully connected to your faith?

- How committed are you to strengthening your faith so that you can powerfully impact your own life and the life of others?

When we tap into the part of us that knows the Truth about how big we all are, we become powerful and courageous. When we get quiet enough, we can tap into this part of ourselves that can see the bread crumbs in the forest, knows which path to follow, and knows exactly what decision to make. By developing this part of ourselves, we get brave. When we tap into the part of us that knows all is well, we vaporize the worries, anxieties, and doubts that get in the way of our glory. We move despite fear, and sometimes experience moments without fear at all. It is a brave new world.

Our intuition is the part of ourselves that knows the answers to our questions. It tells us "nope, no way," "not yet," "maybe never," "it doesn't matter," or "keep your head up!" It's the part of us that giggles at us when we are too wrapped up in our heads, that comforts us when we are too controlling or resentful. It's the part of us that is ever so calm, and says "yes, go ahead," "definitely!," so we can move forward with ease, confidence, and power.

Start to develop your ability to listen to this wiser part of yourself, and follow its guidance. This is where your power is. The more you do this, the stronger your intuition will be — the stronger *you* will be.

The stronger your intuition becomes, the more momentum you will gain; the faster and with greater ease things will happen for you; the more meaning you will see in every moment; the more you will relish your life; and the more you will live in Full Color and inspire others to do the same.

Freedom is possible!

On Mindfulness

> *Quiet the mind, and the soul will speak.*
> *~Ma Jaya Sati Bhagavati*

Our minds, if we are not aware, can be a wild monkey. It can swirl with dissatisfaction, disappointment, annoyance, resentment, and blame. And it can be so easy to fall into this "monkey mind" trap of the ego. The danger of this monkey mind is that if left unbridled and wild, we cannot tap into our full power and intentionally create a fulfilling life or legacy that impacts our communities and the world.

We all engage in this monkey thinking. At times, my monkey mind is honed in on daily routines with my husband and who is responsible for our toddler. So, in the mornings, if I don't stop it, my monkey mind is on the hunt, ready to point out *all* the things that my husband is failing to do for our son. My mind keeps track of all the ways that things are wrong from my limited perspective. And I keep precise count in my mind of how many evenings in a row that I have "had" to take our son up for his bedtime bath and routine by myself because my husband was continuing his nap from earlier in the afternoon or taking a shower or working late.

If I am not vigilant, I could begin and end each day with resentment, annoyance, and feminist self-righteousness. And even as I write this sentence, I can feel the effects of the hormones in my body that are produced as a result of this type of thinking.

One day, I realized that no matter my husband's actions, I cannot start each day and end each day in this way. It harms my own well-being, my body, and my ability to build my business and write this book. Most importantly, it harms my marriage. My relationship with my husband is one of my top priorities, so this type of thinking won't work. For all of us to be our most effective and authentic selves, we need to retrain our monkey minds to stop this wild and unbridled thinking.

So, how do we retrain our minds?

Becoming aware of our thought patterns is the first step. When we become aware or conscious of our thoughts with detached curiosity, we can have great compassion for ourselves and our monkey mind. We acknowledge our own emotions. When unproductive thoughts are ready to leave, we can let them go. Simply the awareness and acknowledgement of our delusional thinking can soften its grip. Just like we soften when we feel heard by others, our monkey mind lets up when we observe it with kindness.

Gratitude practice
What we focus on grows! By cultivating our gratitude, we attract more things for which to be grateful. Gratitude has physiological impact on our bodies. We activate different hormones in the body, happy hormones like

oxytocin, which ultimately produce different emotions, behaviors, and results.

So, here is what I came up with: I am so thankful for my husband's health, for his beating heart, for the blood in his veins. I am so thankful for his lovingness and his love toward our son and me. I am so thankful that he takes out the trash and shovels the driveway after blizzards. I am so thankful that he showers. I am so thankful that he is able to get good rest. I am so thankful that he tries. I am so thankful that his body does what it needs to do. I am so thankful that he works. I am so thankful that he is dedicated to his work and to our family. I am so thankful that he does his best all the time. I am so thankful that I get to spend precious time with my son as he goes to bed. I am so thankful that my son is healthy and happy, and that he has clothes to put on in the morning. I am so thankful for these challenges that help me get clear about the balance I seek. I am so thankful for the opportunity to practice mindfulness and gratitude. I am so thankful that I get to practice unconditional love. I am so thankful that this house is empty right now so I can write this book.

EXERCISE: Put this book down and grab a friend. Let your gratitude pour out as your friend acts as a witness. If you don't have a live human, go into your journal with gratitude. List everything and anything you are grateful for. How does that feel?

Meditation

Meditation is a powerful and lovely way to observe the mind's wild waters. Meditation gives the mind space to race around when it needs to, and help it find calm as it is ready. Our mind is one of the most POWERFUL tools we have at our fingertips. We simply need to discover how it works!

The trick with mindfulness is to be gentle. For new meditators, relax and be easy with it. There is no need to put pressure on your mind to control your thoughts. In the beginning, simply breathe, and observe. There are many online resources, including: recordings of guided meditation, meditation music, online meditation communities, as well as meditation apps.

Here are the basics. Sit comfortably on a pillow or chair. Lengthen your spine. Hold your head naturally, nice and tall, with your shoulders down. And relax: be soft, gentle, and kind.

Start to notice your breathing. Are you breathing from your chest? Or from your belly? If you are breathing from your chest, try to shift your breathing down to your belly. Have you ever watched a baby breathe? They instinctively breathe from their bellies. We all did this. At some point in our lives we forgot how to breathe fully; we got tense and shifted our breath up to our chests, away from our bellies. To return to this natural state, we need to retrain our bodies to breathe from the belly. Meditation helps us do this. So, feel your belly expand on the inhale and deflate on the exhale. Relax. Using the breath is an amazing way to focus the mind because our breath is constant and rhythmic.

Breathing in this way also activates our parasympathetic nervous system. This system counters our fight or flight stress response. Controlled breathing, in other words, helps our body to relax, to relieve stress and anxiety, and to regulate our heart rate and other bodily functions.

Let's try. As you inhale, breathe into your muscles. As you exhale, release any tension you are holding. Feel your muscles relax with every breath — your head, your eyes, your face, your jaws, your neck, shoulders, back, all the way down your spine, torso, hips, and legs. Release all tension.

As you breathe, notice your thoughts as an observer.

Notice the space in between your thoughts.

Be gentle. Keep your mind on your breath, and don't try to control anything. No need to force an experience.

Just breath and connect with your Inner Quiet. Connect with Oneness.

Start small. It gets easier and easier, and more and more satisfying. Try 1 minute. Then 2. Then 3. Try 5 minutes daily for a week, and then grow it to 10. Then 15. Or more.

Do what works for you. It's important to be gentle and not force anything.

As you develop an ongoing meditation practice, you will be able to tap into this Quiet throughout your daily life, including when you feel your emotions boiling over at home or at the workplace. Even a 15-second break and return to Oneness can stop and slow unproductive thinking. In just 15 seconds, you can shift from stressed and overwhelmed to at ease and calm.

The mind is an incredibly powerful mechanism, if we just hop in the driver's seat. When we tame the mind, intuition flows.

Listen to Your Heart. Have Some Fun.
When we have fun, when we play, we begin to dissolve our self-imposed fears and limitations, and allow our intuition to soar. Through fun and play, we tap into our intuition, allowing ourselves to be creative and those sparks to fly. We are able to leverage this powerful creativity, innovation, and out-of-the box thinking in all aspects of our life. This includes our work, our leadership, and our legacy. When I notice that people are signing up for new classes, traveling the world, trying new and different things – being creative – that's how I know: we've got a live one!

Fun and play also allow us to break out of self-imposed limitations, and importantly, the societal limitations of unconscious bias and stereotypes. As an Asian American woman, I struggled a lot with believing in my own powerful voice. And the experiences in my family, community, and the world have reinforced the stereotype that as an Asian, I am quiet and have no voice.

The year of the Awakening was one of the most fun years of my life. I followed my heart. I was 100% committed to whatever my heart desired.

That year, I signed up for voice lessons. Here's why.

Growing up in New York City, my spirit had always been moved by powerful, soulful, and mostly African American vocalists. There is something so visceral that happens when an artist uses their own body as an instrument to resonate and powerfully express human experience and the human condition. For me, given my life experiences in communities of color, it was most powerful when voice and music served as the raw artistic expression of communal pain, tragedy, and power. For me, the use of voice in this way was a certain kind of alchemy. And it was a powerful alchemy that I could resonate with, but that I did not have access to.

As a teen, I was a member of the CityKids Foundation Repertory Company. My vocals were not very good. Honestly, I think my membership was a result of the need for diversity on stage. Despite my mediocre singing skills at the time, I had access on a weekly basis to experiencing vocal power that shook the soul.

Through my mid-twenties, one of my favorite things to do was to hang out at Fat Black Pussy Cat in New York on Thursday nights to listen to my favorite local band. Experiencing live music was how I reconnected with myself, my spirit, and my closest friends.

Most of these performances were by Black artists. Growing up, I listened to R&B, soul, and hip hop, and even had an aversion to the "White people music" that my private school classmates listened to.

My experiences with pop culture just reinforced even more the stereotype that Black people can sing, and I can't. Throughout my exposure to the arts, I held an unconscious belief and stereotype that the soulful people in the world who could sing were Black, and that since I was Asian, I couldn't sing. It was that simple. I honestly believed that because I was Asian, my pipes physically didn't work that way.

Well, it's no accident that the difficult relationship of my late twenties was with a Black musician, a singer-songwriter who used to perform in Dupont Circle. I deeply respected how he pulled passion, desperation, anger, and emotion from the depths of his spirit and released it for us to witness, so publicly. It was powerful raw alchemy. I went to watch him to find release and comfort, and ease the loneliness I felt. My loneliness resonated with the pain of his expression. It was during my quiet time that I would spend reflecting and sitting on my own by the public fountain. I never had a romantic interest in him for many months. I would go listen to be by myself.

When we started dating, I would enjoy his music as his partner in romance and business. I booked him show after show, but we would argue so much, so quickly that the relationship disintegrated, and soon enough, the music stopped altogether.

After my Awakening, I decided that enough was enough.

It was time to finally use my own voice.

I signed up for singing lessons. I learned the bel canto style of Italian opera. I challenged myself to share publicly, and sang two pieces at a student recital. The tone, loveliness, range, and power of my voice surprised me. My body surprised me. I found freedom and movement, and spaciousness in my voice, my belly, my face. I explored my own depth and expression, and finally performed my own public alchemy through my voice.

Additionally, I asked my friends who were in an indie-rock band if they would sing with me for my 30th birthday. It just so happened that three members of the band were Asian American. I booked a local community art space. That milestone birthday was the most intentionally that I have ever celebrated myself. It was the first time in my adult life that I shared authentically and vulnerably with people from all areas of my life — personal, social, work, and community. I invited all people with whom I wanted to reconnect. About eighty people showed up to pack the house.

Together, we sang the band's original music. They even let me do a solo as part of the set.

I sang Adele's version of "Make You Feel My Love." I dedicated the song to myself. Tears came as I sang from my Higher Self to my earthly self.

That was the year that I finally found my voice.

Radical Authenticity
Our intuition has no time to be confused by our lies and masks. We don't have to share everything with everyone. Not everyone is in a place in their journeys where they can accept our Truth. We can use our discernment. However, when we do speak, let's tell our truth fiercely and fearlessly.

When we lie, even small lies, like posting a happy life on social media when we are miserable, we are taking jabs at our authenticity and dimming the light of our souls. We are giving a message to ourselves that where we are now is not okay, that it is ugly and shameful, that we must hide ourselves from others lest we get rejected. When we lie, we judge ourselves harshly. When we are dishonest, it is because we haven't yet fully accepted ourselves.

Take these impulses to hide as signposts on our journey toward radical authenticity. Here! This way! There is shame left over here! In this corner! Clean this up! There is more to heal here! There is light to shine here!

Then, listen to these signposts and begin to do the work. Accept yourself deeply, completely. And little by little, following your Guidance, begin expressing *your* Truth. Trust your intuition. Listen to it. It will tell you what you are meant to keep for yourself and what you are meant to share.

EXERCISE: Set aside some time for some reflection and journaling. Be very kind and gentle with yourself as you answer these questions.

In what areas of your life can you be more honest? With others? With yourself? At home? At work? In the community?

What skeletons are you still hiding in your closet?

What are you still ashamed of?

What regrets, if any, do you have?

How can you learn from those skeletons, accept them as gifts, and let the shame go?

Develop Your Own Guidance System.

Pre-Awakening life is filled with doing things just because other people are doing it or expecting it. While I was on the Hill, after Barack Obama was elected President, many young Democratic staffers started to throw their hat in the ring for political appointments. I did the same, but not because I knew what it meant to be a political appointee. I barely knew what the options were, and few people were around to explain it. I just did what everyone else did, and what mentors suggested that we all do.

So, I examined the list of possible titles that sounded respectable yet attainable. While I was driven to make social impact, I was not seeking to become a political appointee for this reason. I was doing it to create a life that my community and mentors could be proud of. I was doing it to be a "good," "powerful," "ambitious," "respectable," "accomplished," and "committed" leader in the community. I saw myself as a freedom fighter, hell-bent on getting the Asian American community's voice at the table. It didn't matter that I was a "crazed" freedom fighter. I thought I was making social impact. It did not yet occur to me that there are millions of ways to make impact and create a life that was fulfilling.

Now, don't misunderstand me. Everyday, I help clients tap into their intuition and discover their big dreams. Oftentimes, their dreams may very well overlap with what the world defines as success. Personal goals and dreams do not have to be separate and distinct from those of society's. What is important is that no matter what we decide, we are following our gut and making personal decisions on our own terms.

But too often we are bogged down by pressures of our families, our communities, our professions, and our society. We get so constrained by these pressures that we don't make space for our own Voices and authentic desires. We fail to realize that we have wisdom from within to receive. We look externally for answers instead of trusting our instincts, our gut feelings, our own intuitive decision-making abilities. We seek answers from others, and make decisions big and small based on what others advise, creating goals that are not our own or even losing the ability to decide what we want to eat for dinner!

One way to start building your intuitive muscle is to start small. Start by following your gut instincts for seemingly "small" decisions. When walking down the street, follow your gut on where to go, where to turn. Decide on whether to take meetings and just go with your instincts. Decide what food you want to eat. If you have a gut feeling to just post something on social media or write to an old friend, just do it. Make decisions fast, and trust your first instinct.

The more you do this, the more powerful your instincts will become. The more powerful your hunches become. The more synchronicity you will experience. The more you will go with a powerful Flow that is connected to All Things.

EXERCISE: In what areas of your life are you led by others' expectations, and others' definition of success? In what areas of your life would you like to strengthen your own internal guidance system? How would you like to develop your own instincts, and connect with your own authentic desires?

Follow Your Hunches
Our hunches are powerful.

I am Senior Vice President of *CoachDiversity Institute*™. When my business partner, Dr. Towanna Freeman and I first launched the business and were working on filling our inaugural class, I got an instinct to email someone I hadn't spoken to in years about the opportunity to enroll. When I connected with her, I found that it was perfect timing, and now she is one of our students. I had a similar hunch to invite a former client, who won two coaching sessions with me at a community raffle. She had never ever expressed interest in becoming a coach. I followed my "random" instinct anyway. A week later, after no response, I followed yet another hunch and sent her a reminder email. That day, she referred a friend, who then signed up. These hunches didn't come as guesses, they came as instructions. Our instincts and hunches are messages from the part of ourselves that is connected to and knows all things.

When I remember, I power all my decisions with my instincts and my intuition. When I feel crazed, impatient, stressed, worried, or scared, I know I am not using my power. That power allows me to relax, trust, and go with the Universal flow.

Ask quick "yes" or "no" questions
In addition to following hunches, another great way to develop your intuition is to ask your Higher Self quick "yes" or "no" questions. When we are first developing our relationship with our Higher Intuition, the sim-

pler the better. The better we are at listening for that one-word answer — "yes," "no," or "maybe," — the more we are developing our capacity to listen to our Inner Guidance.

You can ask: Is it time to reach out to so-and-so? Do I make this purchase? Do I let this particular challenge go? Do I make a right turn here? Is this particular situation going to be OK?

We are trained in our world to follow our logical mind. However, when logic does not lead to an answer with which our gut is satisfied, we start second-guessing our decisions. Logic is a great tool to use. Don't abandon it. However, develop your full arsenal of genius. Develop your skills with respect to your intuition. Listen to that initial gut check and train yourself to go with it.

Give yourself the space to follow your "gut." The more you do, the stronger your intuition will become, and the more things will happen for you with ease.

Write to Your Intuition, and Get Some Answers.
I began a powerful practice of dialoguing with my Intuition during the year of my Awakening. While I was in the 12-step program, I learned about left-handed journaling as it related to "inner child" work.

Journaling with our non-dominant hand is a powerful way to access the right-hemisphere of the brain. When writing with our dominant hand, we tend to think with our left brain, logically, with reason, and in sync with the way we have been conditioned by society to think. By writing with the non-dominant hand, it allows the unbridled, big-picture thinking, wild, creative, free part of you to express itself and its wisdom.
An early technique I used was to write out a question with my dominant hand (right), and then switch hands. I would let my non-dominant hand (left) do all the talking. I would make sure that I wasn't thinking or mak-

ing any effort with my mind. I would clear my mind and let the insights and instincts come through me.

This tip may feel a little strange to you. And I must say, I questioned whether to put this tip in the book because my ego was self-conscious about whether you would think I'm crazy. But after connecting with and listening to my Inner Wisdom, I had to share it. If I didn't trust and listen to my Inner Wisdom, I would be keeping from you this practice that has been life-changing for me. Writing to your intuition is one of the best tips I have to develop your connection with your Inner Guidance.

Write to it. Write to your Higher Self. It is listening to you. It is omnipresent, always there to support you. It is omniscient, holding all the answers you need. It is patiently waiting to finally be acknowledged! And when you acknowledge your Higher Self, your Inner Guidance, it will have so much insight and encouragement to share with you. It will celebrate you more powerfully than you've ever celebrated yourself. It is waiting to love you, and shower you with blessings, encouragement, and celebration.

Try it. Try it. Try it. Be open. You won't regret it.

If you find yourself being judgmental about the process, do something first that helps you relax. Meditate. Enjoy nature. Do yoga. Take a bath. Do whatever you do that takes you out of your mind zone and into your intuitive zone.
After a year or two, I barely had to switch hands before I received intuitive wisdom. I would receive information, insight, and encouragement so fast that I needed to use my dominant hand to keep up with the flow.

Today, this practice still remains at the core of my spiritual practice.

The first message written back to me when I wrote to my Higher Self was the following:

Hello! I Love You! :) <3

EXERCISE: Use materials that inspire you. Find a journal or nice paper, and pen that feels special. Set the mood for dialogue with your Intuition. Light a candle. Do some meditation. Get grounded, focused, and present.

Using your dominant hand, write out a question that you are grappling with.

Using your non-dominant hand, let your intuition share its knowledge and words of encouragement.

Keep switching hands and dialoguing with your Intuition and see what comes.

At the end of the dialogue, thank your Intuition for sharing its deep wisdom.

Interpret Your Dreams

Creating an empowered, inspired life means examining our deepest desires and resistances. It means bringing shadows into light. It means bringing our subconscious forward into the conscious. It means tapping into our subconscious mind to receive messages and insights.

One way to dive in and take a look at our subconscious patterns, to access our deep wisdom and see signposts, is by remembering, documenting, and studying our dreams.

Here's an example of how I learn from my dreams.

The night of January 18, 2016, the Monday night after the inaugural CoachDiversity training, I had a dream. I was leading a training in a hotel lobby. Sandra Oh, Korean-Canadian actor of *Grey's Anatomy* and Oscar-winning film *Sideways*, was one of my students. At the end of the training, she expressed to me that she really enjoyed the class. I graciously thanked her for her comment and then shared with her a silly fact about me. I told her that when I was interviewed by an Asian American blog and asked which actor I would have play me if there were a movie made about my life, (this blog happened in real life), that I had chosen her. She was so gracious. We took a selfie.

During the dream, I felt calm, easy, and relaxed.

What I take this dream to mean: My self-concept has expanded. I've arrived at the next powerful level of myself. I impact real people, even famous people who are just normal people to me now. I impact influential people, and people I look up to. I also take this to mean that anything is possible, and that I am playing a bigger game these days. And, my idea of what is possible has risen to the next level.

This dream was a sign for me that all is well, that the next more powerful version of myself is unfolding, and that I am on path. It was encouragement for me to continue doing what I am doing.

EXERCISE: Keep a dream journal and a writing utensil by your bed. Before you go to bed, set the intention that you will remember your dream in the morning.

First, as you wake, in your half slumber, start to recall your dream, and write as many details as you can remember. They don't have to be recalled in order. Sometimes recalling portions of the dream that you remember will trigger other details. Document the memories as they come.

Next, how did you FEEL in the dream? This is the most important part of dream interpretation. Were you feeling resentful, angry, or anxious? Or were you feeling elated, excited, or ecstatic? Note how you felt. Ask yourself: Does this resonate with anything that I feel in waking hours?

Third, ask your Higher Self: What is the message of this dream? What do you want me to know? What do you want me to heal? How do you want me to grow? What do you want me to do?

Finally, every so often, let's say weekly, read back through past dreams. Are there any patterns? What meaning or insights come up when you review them in chunks?

When you are called, take inspired action.

Live in Daily Reverence & Meaning

Developing our powerful intuition allows us to live in daily reverence and meaning. This daily reverence is possible because there is faith in the larger unfolding of life.

Colorful Leadership™ allows you to see meaning and purpose in everything. It means waking up with utter joy that you are breathing, that you are witnessing your heart beating once again, that you are alive!

Living in Full Color is waking up with unconditional gratitude for another chance to begin refreshed and renewed. It is living in complete awe of the fact that we can use our minds, bodies, and spirits to intentionally create the experience of a new day. It is reveling in amazement that we can feel the way that we want simply by focusing on that which makes us sad, doubtful, or desperate, or that which makes us joyful, motivated, or in awe. We get to choose. What a blessing!

It means gazing at the beautiful sunrises and sunsets with complete reverence that the Earth has made yet another rotation, and the Universe has been held in place yet again.

It means savoring and interpreting and enjoying everything. Everything serves a purpose, even our pain and experiences that don't feel enjoyable: that purpose is our evolution. Oh Universe! Thank you for helping us grow! Thank you for the challenges and delights! Thank you for always believing in our ever expanding potential!

So, welcome to the New You. Here we go!

SEVEN

....

M. is for Mindset

You've done the work to ground yourself in your soul. You've given your-self unconditional love from the inside-out. You've started your work on taming the mind. You've let go of resentments, and worked on for-giveness. You've followed your heart, invested time in creative fun. You've discovered your Inner Voice. Congratulations!! The mindset shifts you've experienced to get to this point are just the beginning of what is possible. So let's take the next important step: getting our mindset right!

MINDSET IS EVERYTHING!
Through my Awakening, I learned that we need to leverage our minds in order to adjust our emotions, impact our behavior, and ultimately, fulfill our dreams. I want to share this gift with you. It's quite simple and beau-tiful:

THOUGHTS => EMOTIONS => BEHAVIOR => RESULTS
How successful you are at creating the life you love, making the impact of your lifetime, and leaving a powerful legacy all depends on your state of mind: who you believe you are, and what you believe is possible.

What hold us back from stepping into our full power are self-doubt, worry, anxiety, and fear. These emotions have a lot to teach us. They point us toward the direction we need to go. However, if we do not tap into these emotions, all they have to teach us remains unlearned. Instead of being our greatest teachers, these emotions become our greatest barriers to believing in ourselves and our gifts, and becoming who we truly are meant to be. They can paralyze us.

As a leadership coach, I know we have unlimited potential. I have seen first hand that the most powerful leaders are ones with a sustained and intentional positive mindset, and thus, an unwavering belief in their infinite potential.

It is from our perspective, our point of view, that everything else flows. What we believe becomes real! If we believe that the world is unsafe, we will view life through that filter, and see proof that our world is unsafe. If we believe our world is abundant, we will filter our experience through that perspective, and see proof that our world is abundant. It is not about ignoring tragedy and pain. It is about making an active choice about how to interact with situations when they arise.

In other words, when we feel stuck, we can choose to find a new way to approach the issue.

It's time to craft a new mindset, a new way of thinking, that allows for inspired thinking and living in Full Color. Coupled with inspiration, a new mindset will allow all you've hoped for to come to you with ease. You'll receive that new career direction or creative project, those speaking engagements and additional streams of revenue, those new people you were meant to serve, that renewed commitment to a relationship.

All of that will come with ease, one day, one month, one year at a time. But to gain that clarity, to get unstuck, we must do the work on our mindset.

So, what's standing in the way of realizing our dreams? The answer boils down to a few key things: 1) what we believe about our vision; 2) what we believe about ourselves and our ability to accomplish goals; and 3) how comfortable we are playing big.

Ultimately, cultivating a mindset of success involves doing the courageous work of exploring the fears, worries, doubts, and inner critics that hold us back; and replacing these with positive, powerful affirmations that when repeated will help us form new beliefs and habits.

Throughout our journey together, I offer positive affirmations that can help us connect with our own power. These may be used in many creative ways. They can be repeated as a mantra during times of challenge. They can be written on sticky notes and placed in visible places that you can see every day, such as on mirrors or refrigerator doors. They can be painted on works of art, and boldly displayed throughout the home.

In this chapter, let's plow through these limiting beliefs and create new, empowering beliefs to try on.

What You Believe About Your Vision

> AFFIRM:
> My vision is amazing.
> My vision is game changing.
> My vision impacts lives.

What is your vision? Take a brief moment to think about what you would like to achieve. Imagine it in *Full Color.* How does it *look?* How does it *sound?* How does it *smell?* What *emotions* does it evoke? *Who* will it impact? What excites you about your vision?

When you think of *your* vision, what do you believe about it? Do you doubt it? Do you half-heartedly put enthusiasm into it? Do you restrain your enthusiasm for fear of feeling too attached? For fear of failing? Do you believe that the vision is not new, innovative, or unique? All of these thoughts are *limiting beliefs.*

Do you believe your vision is awesome? If you don't, it's time to clean up your mindset about your vision!

Each of you has a gorgeous vision of what you want to see in the world. We each have a purpose to fulfill in this lifetime. When you tap into your inspiration and trust your intuition , your individualized sense of self — what your ego believes to be you — is no longer the source of your vision. Rather, you are the vehicle through which your inspiration is shared with the world. It is coming through you.

So, whether you think you are genius enough, wealthy enough, or strong enough, regardless of any limiting belief, your vision is amazing! When we allow our inspiration to flow through us, guided by our intuition, the vision is *always* powerful. And then, the world always stands to gain.

We, our families, communities, organizations, campaigns, and businesses deserve to thrive. To receive your gift, we need you to believe in your vision.

When we change our mindsets and believe wholeheartedly in our vision, the feelings that we experience are expansive. We feel hope, inspiration, joy, and gratitude. Our will is powered with ease, grace, and faith.

My reason for being is to share this precious gift of transformative mind-set with you, to inspire this feeling in you. I often encounter women of color with the most brilliant of ideas. There is no more beautiful a thing than when a woman leader combines all her life experience with all the challenges and struggles of her family and her communities, and creates a grand vision of how she can *and will* make a difference.

One of my clients is a young, Latina woman. She is brilliant, and has for-midable gifts like we all do. She has a background in mapping, as well as a passion for under-resourced communities. Out of her experiences and gifts, she has the most amazing tech idea to connect people with busi-nesses and events in economically distressed neighborhoods through a beautiful, innovative mapping app. Her vision is to drive economic growth and development in low-income communities and communities of color.

In our first call together, she shared her huge vision. But, she also explic-itly emphasized her inexperience and spoke in a small, tentative voice. She hid behind giggles and "do you know what I mean?" I wanted to shout, "NO I DON'T KNOW WHAT YOU MEAN! PLEASE TRUST YOUR INTUITION SO YOU CAN TELL ME YOUR VISION MORE POWERFULLY!!"

She told me about how she sought corporate sponsorships two years ago when the idea was just a seed, and how she believed the corporate big-wigs pushed her around and tried to control her vision. She continued to explain that it had been two years since she stopped pursuing corporate funding because of these experiences. Guess why she was bulldozed? Be-cause she did not have a powerful mindset to match the power of her vi-sion. She had tapped into her inspiration, but had yet to learn to trust her intuition. With that lack of clarity, her confidence was lacking. So, her amazing vision was unable to flow through her and attain its full power.

She then masked her vision with tentativeness, doubt, and insecurity. Her mind got in the way.

What I want so badly is for the leaders in us to WAKE UP! Wake up to the powerful selves that we are. Wake up to the power within us. I want us to speak our ideas and visions crisply, concisely, and boldly. Ours are delicious desires and they deserve to be fulfilled and enjoyed with rapture. Ours are beautiful and powerful visions and they deserve our respect!

> AFFIRM:
> **My vision is absolutely possible.**
> **My vision is meant to be!**

What You Believe About You

> AFFIRM:
> **This vision is for me.**
> **I am a powerful leader and creator.**

This vision was meant for you in this moment in time. If it weren't, you wouldn't have received it.

One of the most important aspects of life and leadership is knowing and owning your worth. We all negotiate our worth in life, and what we believe about our worth is the number one predictor of whether we find fulfillment.

> AFFIRM:
> **I am already good enough.**
> **I am worthy.**

I'm not good enough until... when? A professional degree? A job title? A certification? A certain salary? Will you feel good enough then? I know many wonderful leaders with professional degrees and fancy titles who still do not feel good enough. The truth is you are already good enough. The moment you believe it, you commit to the vision that matters to you. All of a sudden, things go into motion, you begin to implement your plans, and a whole new world appears. I promise!

AFFIRM:
I am courage.
I am creativity.
I am innovation.

You might have a limiting belief that you have to play it safe to be "successful." Here's the thing. Our world doesn't need more safe, "successful" people. We need new solutions to old problems. We need bold, joyful visions, courageous ideas, and new ways of relating to each other. If you truly believe this, you have no choice but to overcome your fear of judgment as different or even quirky, and step into your power to be a brave trailblazer.

As Albert Einstein said: "No problem can be solved from the same level of consciousness that created it." I know you have amazingly creative solutions to our world's problems inside you. So, let them shine!

AFFIRM:
I am worthy of my vision.
I am worthy of my dreams.
My vision and my dreams were made just for me.

ACK! We might believe that our vision is a good idea, but lack the confidence to execute it. If you don't believe you deserve it, that you are worthy, don't be surprised when you are unable to make your dreams come true. How can we create a beloved community if we don't believe that we ourselves are beloved? We don't want anyone else to limit how big we play — so why should we limit ourselves?

Let's take a look at some examples.

I have a client who was told by his father that not much was expected of him, particularly in the area of pursuing advanced professional degrees. What do you think happened? His mindset was impacted. He set low expectations of himself and had limited self-worth. In other words, he was tentative about goal-setting, and didn't believe himself worthy of achieving goals that he really did want. One of his passions was teaching young minds. He did pursue his master's degree, and completed all of his coursework, began his final paper, but was never able to finish. With this clouded thinking and low sense of self-worth, he left a trail of unfinished personal and professional goals.

Another example is a super-smart African American woman that I worked with. When she was in grade school, her class had a lot of Asian American students. One time she had the highest score of the entire class for a math test. After the tests were graded, her teacher — problematically buying into a multitude of racial stereotypes — brought her up to the front of the classroom. She stood up proudly, only to have the teacher say to the whole class, "Never again should this student have the highest score in the class." It devastated her. In adulthood, she was an extremely high achiever. However, she never did her very best. She didn't remember the incident until adulthood, when she was examining why she didn't always bring her best self, and instead performed well enough to fly under the radar. It was no longer working for her.

In my own experience, as an Asian American woman with a petite frame and the youngest child, one of my biggest struggles has been not feeling "important" enough. At a deep level, I didn't believe I was important. And so when I perceive that others are not respecting my "importance," that causes stress. In reality, people are not spending time thinking about me or my worth. Through my own perception, I cause my own stress. With this broader perspective and acknowledgment, I am able to move through these times of stress, past a sense of victimhood, remembering that I am connected to the Source, and thus capable of greatness.

Those around us, our families, and our communities will impact our mindset. It is only human, particularly when we are in our formative years. However, it is our choice to notice when our mindset is impacted, to discover what limiting beliefs we have been taught. And, it is our choice to reclaim our minds and the direction of our thoughts.

When we know our worth, nothing can stop us.

Quit Playing Small

> AFFIRM:
> I am big and bold.
> I am expansion.
> I am constantly becoming the next, more powerful version of myself.
> I matter.

We create the world around us. If this is true, how do we get in the way of own success? How does our own self-perception limit our ability to build and lead a community that inspires?

Think of yourself as a movie projector, with the camera as your brain, the screen as the world around you, and the image that you see as your experience. In other words, what we see is just a projection of what's in our minds. The film that is running through our camera — our "inner world" — makes all the difference in what we experience on screen — our "outer" world. How we interpret the world *is* what we see and experience. Before our Awakenings, we view what's on the screen and take it at face value. We react to the projections of our own thoughts, as if we didn't create that experience ourselves. We are walking around not realizing the power of our minds as the movie projector.

So, what we experience in "real life" is simply a reflection of how we view ourselves. Amazing!!

How you view yourself IS how the world views you.

]Let's ground this in some examples.

I used to work as legislative staff to a Member of Congress. I am about 5 feet tall, Asian American, female, and an attorney. I had a position of influence and was good at my job. That year, a new staff member joined the team. He was very tall, White, male, and pursuing a doctorate degree. During his first week on the job, the two of us were on the floor of the U.S. House of Representatives. It was my first time on the floor, the lights were bright, and Members of Congress surrounded us. I felt so out of place. Having been a staff member for the prior 3 years, never in a million years did I think that I was someone capable of introducing herself to a Member of Congress. Here was this new staffer, a few days into the job, standing tall. He very simply excused himself, and walked right up to a Member, introduced himself, expressed admiration for a policy initiative, and carried on a normal conversation. I will never forget that moment. It opened my eyes to how differently people perceive themselves.

Some might respond thinking "oh, the arrogance" or "oh, the privilege." Yes, racial, gender, and physical privilege exists. I stood there, not thinking to myself that the world is discriminatory and unfair, but with my mind blown. I wasn't angry at how large he perceived himself. Rather, I became super aware of how small I perceived myself. It was in that moment that I began to see greater opportunity. And then, what was possible for me expanded exponentially.

Don't hold back: share the real you, your passion, gifts, and talents. That is how you will open doors for yourself, step into the new powerful you, and make impact for others.

But also, open your mind to seek out the real in others, their passions, gifts, and talents, even when they don't see themselves as "big."

Later that year, I was selected to be executive director of the Congressional Asian Pacific American Caucus (CAPAC). For many years, I knew a young man about 5 years my junior who often attended political events. After my promotion, when I saw him, he would joke about how I was "big time" now that I was serving as the executive director of CAPAC. At various events, he would motion as if to brush my shoulders off, a gesture that originated from hip-hop artist Jay-Z's hit single *"Dirt Off Your Shoulder."* The gesture is meant to brush off the jealousy of others when one has achieved high status or success.

This felt strange and awkward coming from an acquaintance at a professional networking event. Intuitively, what I sensed from him was a feeling of smallness and insecurity as a young professional. He wasn't playing big or owning up to the seriousness, the power, and the resources within himself. He was not sharing his powerful story. For many years, I did not know one single piece of authentic information about this young man. In his professional interactions with me, he did not emphasize his gifts as a leader. He never shared openly about who he was.

Years later, we had the chance to get to know one another better at a one-on-one lunch. In this more intimate setting, I had more time to probe. He told me his incredible story as an Asian American male growing up in the Middle East, and how that shaped his passion for progressive women's issues. At that time, I told him how incredibly powerful his story was, and encouraged him to allow THAT to be his powerful personal brand. I pushed him: why was it that I did not know this until now? Until that moment, he didn't share what a funny, interesting, and genuine person he was.

How we interact in our professional and personal networks is impacted by our understanding of ourselves and how big or small we see ourselves.

Recognize the power in you, and you will share that power with the world.

Be bold! Be YOU!

EXERCISE: Take a moment to reflect upon the times in your life when you play big and when you play small. With whom do you choose to show the REAL, confident you? Why? With whom might you hide the real, big you? Why? In what situations do you view yourself as big? As small? How would you like to change your self-perception to match your vision, goals, impact you want to leave behind?

Here are two poems I wrote about how BIG we truly are.

Enjoy!

MATTER 2

Two birds in conflict.
One flutters off feeling
i don't matter.
The other alone on the branch
mind spinning round and round, cackling
i matter!! i matter!!
Oh, if they only Knew
how much they do Matter.

MATTER 1

I, matter. You, matter. We are the same Matter.

Arrogance vs. Confidence

AFFIRM:
I stand powerfully in my confidence.

As women of color, we may have been taught humility above all else, and that we should guard against arrogance. This might lead us to believe that we are smaller than we truly are, that we are not important. But the truth is: We are important. We all are important. We are connected to All - That-Is, thus part of divine fabric. This alone makes us each important and gives us the right to stand in powerful confidence. It is our sacred purpose to stand confidently and act upon inspiration and intuition.

India Arie sings:

I am Light.
I am Light.
I am divinity defined.
I am the God on the inside.
I am a star
a piece of it all
I am Light.

We must each tap into this bigness that lies within. This doesn't just impact our lives; our personal empowerment work has ripple effects throughout our communities. We must empower ourselves, or else our visions of personal and community empowerment are a no-go. It is absolutely okay to speak your accomplishments aloud. How else will your friends and family, community, future employer, board of directors, or constituents ever realize what you have to offer to the big picture?

My mother used to call me arrogant all the time. And it used to annoy me, that is, until I was truly grounded in my own confidence.

This topic comes up very frequently when I coach my clients, most of whom are women of color. They often ask how to balance confidence with humility, or how to prevent themselves from crossing the line to arrogance. They say it's a fine line between confidence and arrogance. But I'm here to tell you that it is not a fine line, and that the border between the two is actually a very bright line.

This topic is particularly salient with respect to our attitudes when it comes to the job hunt and our leadership styles. Surely, we wish to feel confident, centered, anxiety-free, without crossing the line to arrogance.

After the Awakening, I was 29 years old. It was only then that I started gaining true confidence in myself. It felt right. I started trusting myself. I also started trusting my gut instincts with a deep sense of faith that I will always be able to handle whatever is put before me, that when the time is right, trusting my gut, that I will always know the choice to be made. My philosophy had shifted to a place where I began to have faith in my journey. I began to trust that every moment is placed before me to teach me something, that every moment is an opportunity for growth and learning, especially those moments that are not wholly comfortable. This trust gave me confidence. And that is exactly what confidence means. "Con-," meaning "with" and the root "fid" meaning "faith." Altogether, confidence is "with faith."

AFFIRM:
I am centered in my divine self.

While I was following my heart, my mother saw it differently. She labeled my new sense of self, and the boundaries and relationship negotiation that came with it, as "arrogance." In her eyes, I was no longer a dutiful daughter, aiming to please her and others Instead, my mother found my actions to be solely self-serving. She interpreted my growth as self-centeredness, and accused me of seeing myself as better than others. There was a cultural lens, I am sure, but it was also a matter of definition. As I was beginning to know myself better, I knew that what I was experiencing wasn't anywhere close to arrogance. And that dissonance, I wasn't able to explain quite yet.

Five years later, I can articulate the difference. Here it is:

CONFIDENCE	ARROGANCE
Security in self as an essential piece of a larger picture	Insecurity in self; overcompensation for these insecurities through dominating, overbearing behavior
Faith - I have complete faith in the future. I know I am evolving and growing as we all are. I know I am always guided and always taken care of.	Fear – I am afraid of the future, and therefore, I need full control over how things happen
Openness	Control
With strong self-concept, I am open to new ideas and learning.	With a weak self-concept, I feel threatened by others and their ideas.

I get it. We live in a society that permits and often encourages arrogance for the dominant culture. As women of color, how do we then navigate the path towards authentic leadership? We can do this by first recognizing the difference between arrogance and confidence. Through confidence we can trust and have faith in our vision. This leads to greater emotional intelligence and more effective leadership.

So here's a question: how do you distinguish between arrogance and confidence?

What do you observe about a person who comes across as arrogant to you? It might be that the manner in which they share their accomplishments feels inauthentic. Perhaps it feels self-serving. Or it might feel like they are not in alignment with the values they purport to have. This is because they are overcompensating due to their own insecurities.

Now, think about someone who conveys confidence to you. In what ways have they communicated their vision? Do you feel you are able to share and exchange ideas freely with them? How do they make you feel? Chances are this person is someone you admire and respect, someone whose vision you might even share or want to help realize, someone who inspires you — a leader. You too have the power to inspire, to lead in Full Color.

You see, there is a bright line between confidence and arrogance. When we are authentic, there is no room for arrogance. If we do our work to stay grounded, alert, and conscious, there is no chance that we slip into arrogance. Our values remain intact, our vision manifests as beauty, strength, and confidence.

Be yourself, and you will shine through. – not arrogance.

Clearing Out Worry and Doubt

Our worries, doubts, and fears are of our own making. We have fabricated them, and as such, we have the power to unmake them. It's time to take a look at our fears, to question and poke holes in them. If we are truly worried about something, create a plan to tackle it head-on. Take your excuses away.

If we allow fear and doubt to sit with us for too long, they become self-fulfilling prophesies. I am working with a client, a Latina who is very accomplished in her political career. As a staffer, she has reached the pinnacle of DC success, and has worked for the White House. Despite these accomplishments, she has struggled throughout her life with weight management and abusive workplace environments. At this point in her life, she is burned out, and wants something new.

However, despite this desire, fear and doubt is plaguing her and preventing herself from making space to dream and to brainstorm. She is unable to create space to find answers, and develop a plan of next steps because she is plagued with fear and doubt about applying her current skills in a new line of work. She is clearly accomplished, intelligent, and capable. However, every answer she gives herself when asked what it is that she really wants is filled with doubt. Rather than asking herself, "How will thinking about my ideal work culture help me in looking through job descriptions?" she tells herself, "This perfect position doesn't exist for me." She is stuck.

Like FDR said, "The only thing we have to fear is fear itself." It creates a self-fulfilling prophesy. Because she is fearful, she is having a tough time even dreaming about what ideal work means for her.

Last year, my business partner and I launched the first-ever coach institute whose mission it is to empower diverse communities through coaching. We sit at the historic intersection of coaching, personal development, diversity, and social progress.

In the months prior to the opening of *CoachDiversity Institute*™, I asked the Universe to fill the seats of our inaugural class with amazing, tuition-paying students. Each day, God told me, "I got this. I got this. Don't worry." He assured me that we would bring in enough to cover costs of the venue, pay our teachers, and have some left over to support our families and reward our hard work. Time and time again, He said: "Don't worry. I will fill the room."

I kept praying, and doubting (which is so human). I hedged my prayers. Like: "Lord, please fill the room with 10-15 students, or better, whatever you think better means for us." I handed it over, and told Him that I would accept less.

Our registration deadline was January 8, 2016. Around Christmas time, reminders had been sent out, emails and calls made. But we still didn't have any firm commitments to enroll. My partner, being a systems genius, started saying things like: "At what date do we decide to cancel?" I understood her concerns. She needed to know, so she could cancel the venue without sacrificing dollars.

In my mind, I was building my faith. There is no way we would need to cancel. God's got this. For the past two months, He has told me every single day! How can we cancel? I didn't even want to entertain the idea to keep my mind clear. I already had some doubt; I didn't need any more!

January 5th arrived and I was on my way to join twelve other powerful women entrepreneurs for a business building retreat. And still, no enrollments. We had a lot of maybes and soft commitments, some interest for the next cycle, but no firm enrollments. No credit card swipes.

I decided to let it go. God told me by the deadline, we would have our students. I handed over the enrollments to God, stopped staring at my inbox, and focused my energy on the retreat.

The retreat was out of town. So, I had the opportunity to move someplace else both physically and mentally, to remove myself from the energy of doubt. I read inspiring books and connected with my Reverence for All-That-Is, and the delight in every moment. I could feel excitement and a natural high brewing within.

That night, something changed. Perhaps it was a new city, new hotel room, travel out of my daily working space. Or maybe it was time alone, reading for pleasure, uninterrupted by family responsibilities. Or it could have been convening with committed, faithful, and inspiring women entrepreneurs. Maybe it was all of the above. I'm not sure what caused that shift. Whatever it was, that night I started trusting in the Divine. The moment I welcomed trust, my doubt and fear disappeared. I started feeling deliciously in tune with everything that was around me. Every moment was a delight.

At the beginning of the retreat, one of the first things our coach worked on was our mindset. This demonstrates just how important mindset really is. She instructed the class, "Write down your biggest fear." That morning, by 10:00 a.m., I already knew what my response would be: I had no fear. Fearlessness. What a blissful and joyful state of being. I was delighted!

During a break, I went upstairs and checked my email. And just like that, at 10:03 a.m., a student had written us about enrolling, and was asking about processing her payment. By around 3:33pm, our second enrollee was signing her enrollment papers, and emailing them to me. I quickly forwarded the good news to my business partner to beef up her faith. Subject line: BOOM!

By the end of our training weekend, we had nearly double our target number of enrollees, and we met our financial goal that God had told me not to worry about!

More importantly, the students were a perfect fit for us. The caliber of students was more than I could have dreamed. Our class included community activists and leaders, a senior political appointee from the Obama Administration, a woman who runs the diversity shop for all the U.S. Senate Democrats, a former NFL player, an international development lawyer who wanted to bring empowerment coaching to work into development, millennial startup entrepreneurs, and a human resource professional.

The quality of our dialogue, conversation, and learning was historic and unmatched. The students entered the inaugural weekend as strangers, and walked away as family.

When we are fearless, the Universe responds quickly. It's time to do the work of looking at our fears, worries, and doubts. Every time you have a worry or doubt, flash a BIG RED STOP SIGN in your mind. The fear is a figment of your imagination. Remove this fear and doubt, and instead allow your imagination to point you toward your voluptuous dreams.

Thank your fear for being a signpost, and take the next step forward.

EXERCISE: Choose an area of life where you feel stuck. In your journal, one at a time, dissect each worry or doubt that you currently have when it comes to that area of life. Pick each one apart. Examine it like an objective scientist would. Poke holes through each one. In what ways is that worry or doubt not true? In what ways is the opposite true? When in the past have I conquered a similar fear? What qualities do I have that make this fear ridiculous?

What new affirmation can I work with to counter my doubts and worries? To fulfill our ginormous visions, there is no room for petty, little doubts. So, at the end of your journal entry, write your prayers and requests, and affirm for yourself a new belief.

For me, the doubt was: "We won't enroll any students." "My family will have a tight financial month." "This is going to flop." "We are going to teach to an empty room."

My affirmation was: "I powerfully attract people and resources to this historically important vision. We will attract the students that are meant for us. We are the answer to their prayers, as they are the answer to ours."

What are your prayers and requests? What is your affirmation?

THE SEED NEVER WONDERS

> The seed never wonders
> whether it will sprout
> Imagine a little seed
> frustrated because it isn't yet a flower
> in full bloom
> A seed is never saddened because others
> do not find it beautiful or super
> preposterous!

Colorful Leadership

A seed never feels poverty or lack
never complains about the soil or the rocks
It sits silently
powerfully
not trying
but being
preparing
waiting
not waiting
for that moment
of breakthrough

A seed never wonders whether it will be more than it is
Never wonders whether it is right or wrong
Never wonders if it is a life wasted
Never tries too hard
nor moves too fast
A seed doesn't judge itself
or compare its own body, shape, and triumphs
to those of other little seeds
A seed doesn't even mind its own business

it just is
it just grows or doesn't
in the right environment
it starts
it feeds
grows roots
finds water
finds light
it has everything in it
has all the power

Letting its own beautiful intelligence
unfold
do it's thing
We are designed to be magical
to grow
to move toward the light

It is our programming
Just like that little seed
there's no doubt
and with that knowing
on our own time
on our own pace
with readiness we sprout
whether planted in rich soil or harsh conditions
we choose the soil of our minds
receive nourishment in all forms
receive water from the heavens
in a space where there is no time
no waiting necessary
we sprout

-    Me/GSC
     2015

Letting Go of Perfect

AFFIRM:
Life unfolds perfectly.
I am perfect, even with my "imperfections."
I am kind to myself.
I remember my Divinity.

In my twenties, I wasn't aware of it at the time, but I was truly obsessed with whether or not I was perfect enough. Even as a values-driven and purpose-driven woman, I was guided by how I wanted the men in my life to view me. I was guided by how I wanted my "profession," the legal profession, to view me. How did I even end up in this field? I had wanted and planned on a career in public policy. A mentor had suggested I take the legal route. I thought to myself, "Sure, why not? That sounds strategically smart," not realizing the full extent to which I was signing up for an entire profession.

A lot of times, we get stressed because things aren't going exactly as we planned. Let go of the need to have a "perfect" or perfectly planned experience. Your experience is already perfection. Let go of expectations. Instead, like a surfer, ride each wave as it comes, find balance, and become an empowered actor who is one with the experience, and co-creates through awesome, relaxed, confident performance. Embrace and enjoy the bumpiness. Smile.

As a leader, you are a trailblazer. But you have two options. You can stress out and pick on yourself and your team for not doing this "right" or that "right." Or you have option number two: you can be gentle with yourself, and those around you. You can accept that you are on an amazing adventure, blazing trails, celebrating small victories, and enjoying that bumpy, but awesome ride.

Perfectionism has served a great purpose. It has been useful. It has protected me. It has conditioned me for excellence in my academic life, and for consistency in high-quality work products in my professional life.

Perfectionism has gotten all of us to where we are now. In many ways, it has protected us from judgment, and helped us receive external praise. But the costs have been high. We gave up our True Selves. We hid the true leader within each of us.

The need to be perfect is fear-based. Think about it. How do you feel when you are constantly judging what you do as not perfect enough? It feels pretty awful, and the results are stagnancy, rigidity, spitefulness, disconnection, and jealousy. It blocks creativity. You can lead others better when they know the real you, and when you know the real you.

After my Awakening, I was 100% committed to living a full life. I was drawn to the arts, and after some coaching, I had a yearning to see what it was like to possibly incorporate the arts into my professional life. I dreamt of having a community arts space, a bookstore, or gallery, with a performance space of my own. My ideal work consisted of hosting performing artists, supporting them, and helping them to build their dreams. After getting some coaching around this, I spontaneously posted on my Facebook feed: "How do you start an art gallery?" A friend of mine who ran a community space for artists replied by offering me a volunteer position to run their art gallery, which hadn't had any life for some time.

Of course I said yes! A few months later, we were getting ready for the first show. The entire process was so far from "perfect" in a perfectionist's mind, but for me, it was perfection.

The artwork didn't start arriving until the week before the show, and we didn't find someone to install the paintings until two days prior. The day of the show, I went to the gallery only to find the track lights in the gallery blew out! So far, this show was anything but perfection. Truly!

But I was not stressed. I was so happy. From that space, I had some inspired thinking.

It was an hour before the show. The musician who was playing the show had just arrived. I quickly asked him if he would give me a ride to the local Target. We did the quickest shopping we could do, and then ran to the check-out counters with ten colorful desk lamps hanging on our arms.

When we set the lights up, the lighting was more beautiful, warm, and creative than anything we could have "planned." The night was a huge success. The sense of community and the love was evident.

At the end of the day, I challenge you to let go of the perfection and judgment that comes with it, and trust that you are exactly where you need to be. Inspiration, creativity, and true perfection will follow.

You are the leader that this world needs right now – just as you are. Do you stumble through your words in meetings? Are you not the most confident person? Are road blocks showing up on your path? Are you terrified by high-stakes phone calls? So stumble! You learn to crawl before you walk. Don't beat yourself up for not sprinting. Remember, one inspired step at a time will lead to a crazy colorful life.

Have fun, and enjoy the process! Know that the world needs your impact right now. And know that your comfort level in your power will strengthen over time. I am thrilled that the best of the best are continuing to work on becoming their true leader within. Together, we can truly heal entire communities.

Here is a poem I wrote when I was so caught up in work that I forgot to stock up on food for my toddler. I was so distressed and felt like an imperfect mom. Enjoy!

THE MOMPRENEUR WHO FAILED TO STOCK UP ON TODDLER FOOD

> Thank you God
> Thank you God
> Thank you God for working Through me.
>
> You can't be everything perfectly

But you can be YOU perfectly
Do that by following your heart
and do that by listening for ME.
I will always tell you you're enough
And remind you of your divinity.

Thank you Lord for listening to me
Who would I be without you?
You never have to be without me
Because you are a part of me.

Thank you Lord for believing in me.
Where would I be without you?
You are so precious to me
Don't forget your divinity

All of my work comes through you
So please know that I need you too
So it's me that wants to thank you
All I ask is keep being YOU.

That is all I have to say now to you
Keep coming back,
I'll always see you through.
This is my promise to you.

Keep being YOU, Keep being YOU.
That is all I ask of you.

- Me / GSC
2016

Who Do You Judge?

Perfectionism is self-judgment. One of the ways our self-judgment plays itself out is through our judgment of others.

We need not beat ourselves up for being judgmental. We all do it. We are human. Instead, I encourage you to notice all the ways that we are judgmental. Through this we can pinpoint the baggage we still carry and identify areas where we can grow.

Those we judge serve as an awesome mirror into the areas of our lives where we may still be harboring resentment, feeling like we haven't gotten our fair share, experiencing a void, judging ourselves, and experiencing any shame around that judgment.

Our judgment shines a light on areas where we still have room to grow. Letting go of that judgment takes courage. The first step is willingness to do the work. So if you are ready, here we go.

EXERCISE: For the next week (or for forever), take note of when you make judgments of others. Many of us aren't even aware of when we do it. One great tool is to keep a judgment journal. When you notice disdain, dislike, or even slight annoyance toward another, whip out your journal and make some notes with complete honesty, without judging yourself. These could be quick notes, or lengthier journaling. If you have trouble, another way to identify personal judgments is to scroll down your social media feeds and notice your reactions.

What do you judge them for?

This is a safe space to be brutally honest. Remember, you are not a terrible person for writing this out! You are not speaking bad things into existence. You are simply doing some detective work for the purpose of self-discovery. Make some notes: What exactly am I judging this person for? Why do I hate them? Why do I have a distaste for this person? What about them annoys me? Most importantly — and make sure to get to this part — what do I actually fear might be true about myself? How might I actually be jealous of this person?

Up until recently, I used to judge women who are outlandishly flamboyant and outspoken. Too often, we are taught to compete with our fellow womankind for attention. And so, I internalized this teaching. These women would annoy me, particularly if I perceived that they did not understand what I have to offer to the world. One of the women I judged was a woman of color who was coaching me on my story. Prior to a coaching session, I just knew that I had something to learn here, and that she was meant for me. Of course, once I looked into it, it was my own insecurity about using my authentic voice that led me to judgment. I coveted the freedom and self-entitlement that she felt to express herself so openly. After all, I had been conditioned to be humble, respectful, and quiet. Once I released this insecurity, and just accepted that I was on the path to my voice, that coaching session was the turning point to this book. I felt that if this radically expressive woman understood me, then I can do this.

Be curious. Find some patterns.

EXERCISE con't: After a week of journaling, see if you notice any patterns in your judgments. Are these people all of a particular gender, age range, or ethnicity? Are your judgments about appearance, money, education, success, or popularity? Where might this pattern originate from? Might it stem from parental, sibling, or other familial relationships? Perhaps in our school environment growing up? Notice what you learn about yourself and your own insecurities. Stay curious, without judgment. In other words, don't judge your own judgments. Notice your patterns without labeling them as "good" or "bad."

In my example of my insecurities around my voice, I can easily point to the origins of that insecurity. Growing up as a girl in a Chinese family and cultural community, I was not taught to speak my mind. I was taught that to keep quiet and polite, and to study rigorously and get high grades in school was to be a "good" girl. This is not to point fingers and blame my family, culture, or upbringing. This is simply awareness about where I come from. I get to choose where to go from here.

We get to choose.

Be Gentle and Forgive Yourself

Take the time to be gentle with yourself, and process any emotions. Our judgment is really just cover for our own insecurities and unresolved pain. Keep at it, and love yourself anyway. We all have insecurities, and there is no need for shame. In fact, take pride that you are doing the work to clear your mind, heart, and spirit.

What Do You Want To Do Differently?

Congratulations! You've taken the time to learn more about your patterns and resentments that you are holding from the past. Let's not stop there! Now, what do you want to do with it? What insights are coming up? How is this holding you back? It is such a gem to know what we are still holding onto, not only for awareness sake, but also for decision-making to move forward.

The #1 question is: now that you are aware, how will you show up differently?

For me, to push past my insecurities, my next steps were to speak up anyway, find my authentic message anyway, write this book anyway. And one day I'll wake up and these particular insecurities will be a distant past. And the very cool thing is, the next insecurity will pop up and help me continue to grow and evolve.

> AFFIRM:
> I thank God for my insecurities.
> They help me in my never-ending growth and expansion.

> AFFIRM:
> Today, I forgive myself for judgment.
> I was not aware, and am always doing my best.
> Today, I am willing to let it go.
> I now know – I am always enough.

Forgiveness is a Key to Freedom.

Another important step to developing a mindset for success is clearing out your thoughts that lead to feelings of resentment and complaining.

We block our blessings, creativity, and sparks of insight when we consistently complain and hold resentments. These chips on our shoulders can chip away at our capacity to keep moving toward our dreams.

Let's take a look at what happens when we complain or judge. When we complain or judge, we are using our words to express disagreement with how our lives are unfolding. We are fighting experiences that the Universe is offering to us as opportunities for growth.

We take the focus off opportunity. How can we learn, grow, and develop if we are putting our energy into complaint and resentment? The same way a focus on opportunity brings more things to be grateful for, the focus on complaints and resentments brings about more things about which to complain and to resent.

In this way, complaints and resentment keep our mind and energy stuck on the problems, instead of solutions. The focus is on what we don't want, and on things we cannot change, leading to more of the same.

Finally, complaint and resentment shut down creative thinking and constructive communication. When we focus on what we don't have, we sharpen and hone our ability to pinpoint what disappoints, annoys, and angers us. We strengthen the muscle of complaint in our minds. When we utilize that muscle over and over, we flood our bodies with hormones that are associated with the thoughts of complaint, and over time, erode our health. This blocks our intuition and flow, prevents us from noticing synchronicity, and ultimately prevents us from being the creators and leaders we are destined to be.

We all can pinpoint those people in our lives who are stuck on playing that record of complaint over and over in their minds. Think of how ineffective they are at creating a life they love. This is not to criticize, but to learn from their choices.

A great way to clear out our resentments and complaints is through forgiveness. We forgive others not for them, but for our own freedom. There is a Buddhist saying that "[h]olding onto anger is like drinking poison and expecting the other person to die."

Forgiveness is a key to freedom.

EXERCISE: Make a list of all the resentments and complaints you have in your life. Grieve the loss of things not going your way. Go ahead. Give yourself room to feel the pain and anger of the disappointment, to process the emotion, possibly for the first time ever. Take as much time as you need.

For each of these resentments and complaints, write letters to those against which you have grievances; write letters to the situations themselves; write letters to the Universe. Give words to how you feel.

Then, send the letters, bury them, burn them, archive them. Wish your grievances well, and bid them adieu. Do whatever you need to release the resentments and complaints. Follow your Inner Guide. It knows what to do.

Meeting Our Inner Critic

Inner critics are the voices in our minds that tell us that we're not enough – not good enough, not smart enough, not desirable enough, that we're not worthy of our dreams. We all have inner critics! There's nothing to be ashamed of!

When I declare that I am ready to do the courageous work of being myself, squads of critics show up. In order to do my work, and make my impact here on Earth, I have to set my intentions and turn them into a cheerleading squad instead.

When I was ready to transition from Asian American and Pacific Islander politics to coaching, the head of my crew of inner critics, my Chief Inner Critic, showed up. I call her Furugula. Her name reminded me of Disney villainesses Cruella De Vil of *101 Dalmatians* and Ursula of the *Little Mermaid*. The fact that it rhymed with "arugula" added a silly factor. The guttural sounds of "Furugula" made me think of how deeply engrained she was in my psyche, and how much impact she had on my thinking.

Furugula was mean and ever-present. Because of her incessant bullying, it took me about a month of cowering in fear before I posted my very first blog post as a new coach, *How Joy Makes Us Stronger Leaders*. I now know that she was only trying to protect me from public humiliation.

But at the time, I was sick of all the internal dialogue. To have a fighting chance, I had to make her come out and face me in broad daylight.

Trigger Warning: I am about to take you into the nightmare that was happening in my mind during the time of my professional transition. Below is a raw, mean, traumatic, custom, mental attack that is nuanced, cunning, manipulative, and desperate all at the same time. This may cause a trigger for those who might be in a particularly sensitive space in the moment. However, for those who are ready to read on and confront your own inner critics, my sharing will help you recognize the voices in your own minds and take seriously the negative impact of letting them run the show. This is a weighty subject. And as such, I am not sugar-coating the letter that Furugula actually wrote to me. Small edits have been made to ensure anonymity.

Letter from my Furugula, my Chief Inner Critic

Dear Gloria,

This is your Chief Inner Critic, Furugula. I see you've done a lot of nice peaceful work to IGNORE ME! Why? For Happiness? That is crazy talk. Don't listen to your coach. Don't listen to that prancing inner child of yours! It's the WRONG WAY TO GO. What are you going to do NOW? Be a LIFE COACH? INSPIRE people to prance around in fields of yellow daisies? **That is NOT how the world works!**
You will NOT be Free! Not under my watch. Please come back and listen to me. **LISTEN TO ME!!**

Listen to you mother. She has worked so hard for you. Who are you to receive financial gifts from her and NOT **DO** and **FEEL** EXACTLY how SHE WANTS? THE NERVE of you to be your own person! THAT IS CRAZY! You are NOBODY. If you take her money, you must DO as she says and FEEL as she directs. Understand? Just suck it up! The relationship is never going to be better! Just take the abuse! Embrace the fear in your heart. Accept it. Always. *You are getting fearful... You are getting fearful... You are getting fearful.* Did it work? Are you filled with fear now?

Oh, and don't even get me started about that job you left. You are such a wimp. You are such a *@$$%! **I DESPISE YOU!!!! I AM SO ASHAMED TO BE YOUR INNER CRITIC. YOU DON'T DESERVE MY HATRED!!!!** You have no backbone – You can't even stand up for yourself! You should be strong, but you are weak! You should be able to withstand the pressure of being an AAPI SPOKESPERSON for the ENTIRE community. I can't believe you are turning your back on your community and leaving your job. You're leaving because you are weak, because you can't handle it. You can't handle the pressure of being a national leader, a national voice. Just as you were getting good at media, at fundraising. NOW you LEAVE?? YOU SUCK!

All these people are disappointed in you. They hate you. Nobody likes you. You're a LOSER and NO ONE will ever want to speak with you again. You are NOBODY. At your old job, you met the President of the United &$^#%@ States! As a life coach, you'll be prancing around with what? FAIRY DUST? Sprinkling the poisonous magic of positivity everywhere!

I'll have so much work to do to clean up after you and your positivity. I hate your vision, your hopes, your dreams. No one will ever care about you again. You will swirl down the toilet of HAS BEENS. You are nobody. Crazy. You're scared of power aren't you? Aren't you!

My name is Furugula and **YOU SHALL LISTEN TO ME!!!!!** Be my slave I say!!!! Be my slave!!!!

I HATE YOU!!!!!

Never yours, never loving you, always hating you,

FURUGULA, THE MEANIE, THE BULLY.

NEVER FORGET ME!!!!!

I need you to survive.

I'm dying. I'm getting weak.

Do you really want me to die and get weak? **I'M STRONGER THAN YOU, meaner than you!**

I am. Don't you love me? Hate me. Love me. Hate me. No, love me.

Let me go. Go away now.

Please, leave me alone.

{Furugula retreats to her dark cave.}

***

As you can see, my Chief Inner Critic had a LOT to say. She was rather intense and very active the week of my career transition. This is not surprising. Our critics fire off most intensely during times of transition. They are totally normal, and show up when we are about to take leaps of faith, and step out of our comfort zone. By nature, these courageous steps have the tendency to trigger self-doubt. Take comfort in the fact that this happens to us all, whether we realize it or not.

But now that Furugula was exposed, it was time to respond. We all have our own unique way of showing up in the world. Similarly, the way we tackle our inner critics will be equally unique.

Here was my response to my Chief Inner Critic:

Dear Furugula,

First, happy Thanksgiving. I hope you are celebrating with loved ones.

Thank you for your note last week. I haven't written back until now, because it took me some time to process what you said.

It is nice to finally meet you electronically. I have felt your presence in my life for about thirty years now, but we never officially met.

In the kind spirit of Thanksgiving, I want to thank you for protecting me all this time. Thirty years! That's a long time to care for someone. I really appreciate your fierce loyalty. With your protection, I made it through high school, college, and even law school, with flying colors and tremendous achievements that I would not have been able to conquer without you. I have degrees from Swarthmore College and Harvard Law School; I served as executive director of a caucus in the US Congress. We have done amazing things together in this partnership.

I sensed in your email that you are fearful that I might no longer need you in my life. I reassure you that I still want you in my life. You are a dear friend, and you know me more than most beings in this world. However, I have changed and matured much in the past few years. **So, I need to tell you: in order for our relationship to work, I need our relationship to change too.**

In the last three years, I have learned a lot about how the world works; what my power is, my truth, my contributions, and my potential. I have grown a lot. Your old ways of protection that you have been using to keep me safe all these years, are no longer working. Actually, they are holding me back, and keeping me from reaching my full potential in this amazing world. I have tremendous gifts. **I no longer need a voice of doubt. I need a voice to protect me from doubt, and to help inspire my continued growth. Will you be that protector?**

You may wonder where this is all coming from. I made a decision in 2009, to unconditionally love and protect myself, and to nurture my seedlings of confidence and love. I no longer collect shame. As I ventured from the Hill to the nonprofit sector, and now in my new career as a coach, I find that I still need a protector. I need a protector from all the nay-saying voices out there and in my own head. I need protection so my true voice comes through, and my True Self shines through, so that I may share my gifts and talents with the world. I hope you come with me on this journey. However, you should know that I will fulfill my purpose in life no matter what, and I will do it with or without your help.

Because I love myself, and I truly love you too. I thought about breaking up with you, but it hurt too much to think about life without you by my side. I hope you consider continuing our partnership. It would be tremendously helpful if you played the role of protecting my True Self from the doubts of my smaller selves, and from the doubting words and skepticism of others.

I sincerely thank you once again for your work, commitment, and loyalty to me all these decades. I wish you a happy Thanksgiving.

With gratitude,
Gloria

So, you see, there is absolutely no need to fear our inner critics. They were actually created to help us, and to protect us from the unknown. As we develop strength and resolve to make peace with our Inner Critics, they will have less destructive power over us.

Plus, they have wisdom to offer us. Our inner critics show up to protect us by maintaining the status quo just when we're on the verge of something powerful and true. Their very presence confirms for us the path of greatest courage. There is wisdom in following that path when the time is right for you.

EXERCISE: Write a letter from your Chief Inner Critic to you. Do some meditation or relaxation beforehand. Take a bath. Take a nature walk. Do something to clear your mind. Then, pick up the writing utensil and let your Chief Inner Critic speak. Let its personality and energy come through. Don't be afraid. Let it be its own authentic self. Take your time.

Then, spend some time to process the letter. As long as you need. I took a week. When you are ready, write your response back to your Chief Inner Critic. Thank it for its service. Acknowledge all the work it has done. Make your requests.

Do what you need to do in order to seal the deal. Follow your intuition. Burn it, shred it, share it, keep it, trash it, bury it, archive it, publish it. Do what you are called to do.

We Help Others Shine.

When we clean out our minds, we let ourselves shine. Our self-confidence will radiate and create opportunities for others.

Communities do not thrive unless its leaders know their own worth and own it proudly. When you showcase your contributions and get that new position, our communities' voices are strengthened at the table. When you ask for more money for your organization with confidence, more resources flow to support the important work that you are doing. When you practice self-care as a parent or caretaker, you ultimately have more to give. When you stand firm in your vision, the movements we galvanize can gain strategic visibility. When you get that raise, you spend less time working multiple jobs, and can focus on what you are passionate about. When you do more than just stay afloat and actually thrive, you can provide critical services to those who need it with ease and joy.

Remember, as leader, both the young and the old will model you. Whether you have expressed anything aloud, they can sense your thoughts and emotions, and learn from your moves. Your staff models your beliefs and your actions. Entire organizations, businesses, and campaigns follow your leadership; that's why believing in your self-worth is fundamental. If leaders don't believe they are worth "it" – whatever "it" is – how can our communities be empowered, model Full Color leadership, and rise to the wholeness that we are seeking?

Now that we've cleaned up our minds a bit, it's time to explore our passion and purpose.

EIGHT

....

P. is for Passion & Purpose

So far, we have covered living with *inspiration*, being guided by our *intuition*, and exploring the power of our *mindset*. In order to truly live life in Full Color, we must tap into our passion and purpose. Living disconnected from our passion and purpose leads to alienation, stagnation, disillusionment, and settling for less than we deserve.

In this chapter, we will explore ways to access our *passions* and discover our *purposes*.

A New Yardstick for Success

Do you measure your success with someone else's yardstick?

Our innate need to prove ourselves can sabotage our fulfillment, in our personal and public lives. Remember, I'm not talking about conventional success here. I am talking about living a life where we feel alive, grateful, powerful, and inspired every day! When we are driven by fear of not being good enough, we can have incredible outward success, and still not be able to find inner success and fulfillment.

External measures of success may give off the appearance of fulfillment and productivity, but do you want a life that just looks good on the outside? *Or* do you want a life that you actually love in the moment, every step of the way?

I know a woman who posted warm photos of her husband and child on social media. My initial reaction was, "What a lovely family, and how beautiful and happy they seem!" But when we talk on the phone, she was always so unhappy: unhappy with her life, her husband, her career, all of it. It saddened me that our public and private lives are so disparate.

Similarly, another woman friend of mine has risen to high stature working for President Obama, and Vice President Biden. She regularly posted photos of herself on social media with these powerful leaders, smiling so brilliantly. But these photos were a façade. I soon got a call from her asking for career coaching. She felt lost and inside, was not happy or fulfilled with this outward seemingly successful career.

Have goals. Goals are important. They drive and motivate us. The problem occurs when those goals are not our own, particularly when they are not connected with our sense of purpose and passion. They may be our parents', peers', or our industry's goals and measures of success.

It is essential to define goals on *your* own terms. What lights you up? What delights you? What give you joy? Make sure these goals are deeply intertwined with *your* purpose and passion. Let what sparks you guide your choices.

Along the same vein, we often make our happiness dependent on *future* goals. You might think, "I'll be happy when I finish this degree, get that promotion, win this election, lose this weight, buy that house, or pay back that loan." But, constantly living in the future can lead to defeat, hopelessness, and insecurity.

We can only enjoy a life in Full Color in the present moment. Find the delight in the present moment. It means finding the Color in every moment. We may have high goals and destinations that we want to reach. However, the truth is, we have already arrived. Life is so deliciously enjoyable and delightful if we just let ourselves enjoy it in the present. There is only the present moment. From our limited perspective, all we have is, right now... and now... and now... and now... The future doesn't exist. Our experience is simply the culmination of present moments. If you want a fulfilling life on all levels, you have to connect to the feeling of fulfillment, delight, and joy, right now, and live each moment in Full Color.

Finding Your Calling

In any given season, we each have a calling or even, multiple callings. As we fulfill each one, we will find deeper and deeper layers of ourselves to explore. We are never finished growing.

It is my deep knowing that our life's work and most profound impact on humanity happen when we follow our passion. When we follow our desires, all true roads lead to both personal fulfillment AND service. Therefore, when we do what delights us, when we "follow our bliss," we are not only benefiting ourselves, we are sending ripple effects throughout the world. With this impact, it is our only obligation to create guilt-free spaces to explore courageously what sparks our passion in our life, and what it is we truly want in this lifetime. When you find your true calling, all of us stand to gain. It's evolutionary!

Sometimes, I meet women of color who feel that given our access to power and resources, we must serve in a particular, limited way. Many leaders I coach believe there are specific measures of success that they must meet regardless of whether these milestones line up with how they are meant to serve or their desires. For example, I thought that given my access to education that I *had* to go to law school, and *had* to be a voice at the table for my community. These pressures stem from cycles of family and community traumas passed on from one generation to the next. So, in our minds, we create goals that may not match what we actually want or how we are meant to serve. Our pressures to serve may be well-intentioned, but we limit ourselves in how we are to serve. We forget that we can feel good while we serve. It doesn't have to be about sacrifice.

I'm here to free you. Our only obligation to our communities and our planet is to create an obligation-free space that honors *us*. By freeing ourselves, we ultimately make positive impact on our families, communities, and the world-at-large. Thus, the cycle continues. As we embrace our own way, we give freedom to others in our communities and beyond to do the same. So, let go of pre-set notions of success and embrace *your own* passions and dreams!

As more people strive to accept their unique passions and fulfill their visions – sooner than later – our human race will continue to evolve for the better. That is why I do what I do. I feel this calling so deeply and urgently that I am building a movement around it.

Join me if it delights you!

Pave Your Own Way
The best way to a life and an impactful career that fulfills you is to pave your own way. Following cookie-cutter paths does not provide much room for reflection. And, defaulting to convention is an easy way to take the back seat and allow others to decide what should bring you fulfillment. This was the path I took when I was a law student.

I knew that I wanted to be a public interest lawyer. I have always cared about building community, inspiring leadership, and the championing ideals of democracy, particularly for minority and underserved communities.

Even still, I interviewed for big corporate law firm jobs, mostly to make my dad proud of me through the six-figure starting salaries these firms were offering. He had raised an immigrant family of four on much less, and I felt the duty to try to make some money to please him. I applied to over a dozen firms, hating the interview process every step of the way. In my mind, I tried to rationalize my way through the interviews. I told myself that perhaps global transactional work would be interesting, and that I could learn a lot. But I was never more inauthentic. As a result, I got one call back, and no offers. While it was one of the most depressing times in life, I am so thankful that the corporate law firm doors were closed, because I would have hated myself and my life in that world.

After I failed to get a big law firm job, I was able to follow some semblance of passion and pursue public interest law. Even still, since I had a law degree, I only saw possibilities in conventional public interest law paths. I felt confined to the literal practice of law. How ironic. I had gone to law school to expand my possibilities, but instead, I felt limited. What was possible in my mind had shrunk down to very specific, pre-approved avenues of law practice. Even though my intention for earning a law degree was to do policy work, I found myself applying only for attorney positions in the public interest sector. I applied to be a city attorney negotiating deals for the City of New York. I applied for a small firm that worked with labor, nonprofits, schools, and housing coops. I applied to work at the Manhattan District Attorney's office, even though I felt uncomfortable with the idea of putting disenfranchised people of color and poor people away to prison. I applied for a housing fellowship as a transactional attorney to create affordable housing. Finally, I applied for anything and everything on Capitol Hill, and thankfully, I landed in a dream office working for Congressman Mike Honda doing public policy work for the Asian American and Pacific Islander communities. Although my career applications were all over the map, I landed with the opportunity that was the perfect fit for me.

Today, my career does not include the practice of law and I love it! As a career and leadership coach, I know that possibilities are limitless for all my clients, no matter what. I assist them in gaining clarity about what they really want, and being intentional as they create next steps towards achievement of their *own* goals. Intentionality is the name of the game.

As a young graduate from an elite institution like Harvard Law School, I felt tremendous pressure to work towards claiming a seat at the table for my community in ways considered worthwhile by society. After all, not many from communities of color or immigrant communities get to where I got. I my mind, I didn't want to be a waste! I was guided by this pressure as opposed to following my guidance and intuition. We all always do the best we can given our level of awareness. That period was part of my life path and helped shaped who I am today. It gave me information to help me discover my passion and true purpose, and helped me develop the resources to help others do the same.

I invite you to reflect on what *truly* fulfills you. Not what others think is fulfilling. Not what fulfills you enough, or is tangentially related to what you set out to do. But what truly fulfills *you*. Do the work. You are worth it!

Analyze Your Life With Detached Curiosity

One of the best ways to find your life's purpose and calling is to examine your past with curiosity. Act as if you are taking your life's experiences to a laboratory, and probe your life rigorously, deeply, with curiosity, and non-judgment. See what you find.

Seek out the parts of your life that have meant the most to you. Discover what purpose your experiences, delights, and challenges have had in shaping who you are. Recall moments of pure bliss, passion, and delight. Recall moments of devastation. Recall your defining moments that made you who you are.

EXERCISE: List the top five defining moments of your life. What gave those moments meaning? What did you love about those moments? What did you learn about your passion? What gifts and talents were revealed? What are you learning about your purpose from this list?

EXERCISE: List all of your current commitments on your schedule. For each one, write what you love about those commitments. What themes and patterns emerge from this exercise?

As I came out of my Awakening, I spent a lot of time nurturing myself and giving myself the space to explore various aspects of myself. Within me, I discovered:

- The Artist
- The Leader
- The Social Change Maker
- The Advocate
- The Inspirer
- The Intuitive
- The Youth Inspirer
- The Connector
- The Community Outreach Genius
- The Teacher

EXERCISE: Make a list of all the various aspects of yourself. Journal about each aspect of yourself and why it moves you, and how you feel when you honor that aspect of yourself.

How to Start? Delight Yourself!

We live our life in Full Color by following our purpose and passion. How do we do this? Follow what delights you! As Joseph Campbell said, "Follow your bliss."

The best place to start is to have fun exploring yourself and who you are. Do you ever notice that friend or colleague that just decided to take up trapeze, or watercolor painting, or cooking classes? Or began performing in a band on the side of their 9-to-5? Or started using the hashtag #365daysofhappy? That's when I know someone is powerfully co-creating a life that they love. People who are committed to living a life in Full Color do whatever it takes to honor that which brings them joy.

EXERCISE: Make a list of ten things that delight you. Then go do them. Rinse and repeat!

Then ask, what do I love? And why? Ask yourself clarifying questions. What do I mean by that answer?

Keep asking until you get to the core of who you are. What aspects of the things that delight you do you love? Why? What does that say about you? How about your hobbies? What home, community, and work experiences have delighted you? What relationships have delighted you and why? What does all of this say about your passion, your strengths, and your purpose?

Remember, you are so special! Nobody can do what you do, in the special way you do it. We, out here in the world, need you. We need you to come home to yourself. We need you to find joy and connect with the wisest part of yourself that knows all things. We need you to live in Full Color, so you can give others the powerful permission to do the same.

You are the only one who gets to create your definition of success. There will always be an excuse to wait: I'll do it when my network and reputation are established; I'll do it when I've finished graduate school; I'll do it when the debts are paid; I'll do it when the kids are grown up.

The truth is, you don't have to wait. You can choose to let go and learn about your passion and purpose now. You can let life delight and please you, now. You can start living life in Full Color, now.

How a "Hobby" Led Me to My Life Purpose (and Why That's Not As Scary As It Sounds)

One way to start creating a life we love is to cultivate our hobbies. Are you an artist? Do you love to sing? Do you like to take computers apart and rebuild them? Take long hikes? Volunteer at the local zoo? Organize and reorganize your closet?

Many people discount their hobbies and pastimes as irrelevant to their life purpose. This is so far from the truth! While you may not feel you have the luxury, privilege or permission to pursue your true passion at full throttle, your passions have a lot to teach you about who you are.

Hobbies give us the most relevant information about what fulfills us.

In our world, people often get stuck in a scarcity mindset. Most families of the past few generations have experienced the struggles and trauma of war, depression, systemic injustice, capitalism, and revolution. These experiences have conditioned us to believe that time, money, and resources are scarce. So our hobbies, or what we do without getting paid, say a lot!

Growing up in New York City, one of my favorite pastimes was to participate in and be around soulful, funky, live music and artistic expression. It took my breath away being around powerful vocalists and musicians who used their own bodies as instruments to express what we all feel. Experiencing live music was how I connected with myself, my spirit, and my closest friends.

After my Awakening, I committed to reconnecting with the arts, with that feeling I used to have growing up. I wanted to understand what it was about the arts that made me feel so alive. I was testing out the depth and contours of my commitment to this passion, and experimented with the idea of making the arts a part of my profession path. I started volunteering at the local gallery and community arts space. I was at a time in my life where "good enough" was not enough. I wanted to live in 100 percent, full commitment to my own Light, to follow my instincts, no matter what the costs.

After months of exploration, I finally decided to take the plunge – to follow my instincts and devote all my energy to my own Light. My plan was to drop everything and become a professional music manager.

I rewrote my resume to highlight my work in the arts, and showcased my communications and political skills in the context of artist management. I submitted my materials to artist management companies to get my foot in the door. After seven years in Asian American politics, I was ready to leave it behind and start anew.

Throughout my Awakening, I hired a coach to support me through my growth. The Universe had sent her to me one day through an arts organization, at a time when I didn't really know much about life coaching.

During a session with my coach, as I was exploring the field of artist management, and it dawned on me that I could care less about helping artists make money, book gigs, or land record deals. I felt as if I had simply replaced one political profession with another.

My coach asked me, "What is it about the idea of music management that inspires you?"

My answer opened me up to my true purpose.

I love helping people find their voice, and reveal their own life's purpose and mission. I love inspiring them to be courageous enough to pursue their dream and share it with the world. BOOM! Once that hit me, I realized that this was the common denominator in all that I did – it was what I also loved about music management, politics, community empowerment work, and youth work. It was what I loved most about everything I had ever done. Period.

Through my hobby, I found my purpose — and a new career.

That insight changed my life, and it is why I started my own business as a career and leadership coach.

When I contacted the coaching school, it just so happened that the admissions staff was a former music manager who changed paths to become a coach, for the same reasons that I didn't want to go into artist management.

Amazing! The Universe sends signs through synchronicity. I was on the right path.

So what is your hobby? And what about it makes you come alive? Determine this, and you may receive powerful hints about your passion and purpose.

Your Life's Work

So, we've done a lot of work together so far in pinpointing your passion! Remember, we continuously grow and change, and as we fulfill a purpose, another pops up.

Here is my special formula for your purpose this season:

> **WISDOM From Life's Experiences Including Challenges Overcome**
> +
> **COMMUNITY & Sense of Belonging**
> +
> **DIVINE GIFTS**
> =
> **The Sweet, Colorful PURPOSE of the Season**

There are three critical proponents to your purpose or calling of the season. They include (1) the wisdom you've gained through your life experiences, including through the challenges you overcame, (2) your community or sense of belonging, and finally, (3) your gifts and talents.

Too often, people on their professional paths may not touch any of these aspects. Or one might satisfy and honor one area or two, but seldom do we hit all three areas simultaneously to find the delicious satisfaction and high impact that is our season's calling.

Let's go through each aspect, one at a time.

Wisdom From Life's Experiences Including Challenges Overcome

The wisdom that we gain through our life's experiences are gifts to us from the Universe! They are also signposts on our journeys to discovering purpose. Particularly, the challenges that we've overcome were tailor-made for us to prepare us to carry out our purpose. We can find great bits of information about our purpose and passion by taking a look at our challenges. One of the thresholds that I crossed in adulthood was transforming my relationship with my Asian Tiger Momma, and learning to speak my truth and be in healthy intimate relationships. Today, I help countless others, particularly women of color, find their True Selves in the face of having been conditioned not to have their own ideas in the family. This work impacts their relationships in their personal lives and in the workplace, and how confidently they stand in their personal power.

Let's look at another example. I know an African American woman who attempted suicide in her 20s, and practiced self-harm. Poetry saved her life. Now, she is passionate about being a voice of hope for others who are struggling with self-harm and suicidal thoughts by sharing her poetry to broad audiences. An integral part of her purpose this season is to give hope to those feeling despair. The wisdom that she has gained is that there is hope in a new day.

EXERCISE: Do some journaling to discover your unique wisdom.

- What wisdom have you gained through your life's experiences?
- If you had one lesson that you could share with your younger self, what would it be?
- What challenges have you overcome?
- What do they teach you about your purpose?
- your passion, your strengths, and your purpose?

Community & Sense of Belonging

Second, our calling for the season is connected with our feeling of community or sense of belonging. It may be women, immigrant and refugee communities, artists, communities of color, rural communities, Native communities, or the global community. Our personal and family histories are often intertwined with communities that need a voice. For example, after I graduated from college, I was certain that I was passionate about empowering the Asian American community, but I just wasn't sure how.

Even today, I almost didn't make this book explicitly for women of color. Thank goodness for some coaching that I received! I thought to myself: this wisdom is universal! Why should I make people feel uncomfortable or excluded by saying this book is only for women of color? The answer is that women of color are my community and where my sense of belonging lies in this season. This is not about separation. It is about service. This is the audience that I am meant to serve for the greater purpose of oneness of humanity. We all have so much growing and moving to do. There is no shortage of people working to reach wider audiences. But, my unique purpose and calling in this stage of my life is to speak directly to women of color and inspire us.

EXERCISE: List the communities and groups where you feel at home. What are the commonalities? Which one resonates with you the most?

Divine Gifts

Finally, what are your unique, divine gifts?

Our unique gifts are so deeply intertwined with our passion. When we tap into these gifts and exercise them, we feel joy, delight, and passion. This is the area that we tend to ignore so much. We ignore who we are in order to fit neatly into professional boxes.

Check this out: just because we are good at something as measured by someone else's standards doesn't mean that that is our *unique and divine GIFT*.

I may have been pretty good at proofreading and preparing legal documents, but it was not my GIFT. It bored the heck out of me. I wanted to scratch my eyes out. There was not one drop of delight or passion. Not one.

My gift is that I am a creative genius. God works through me fast. I compiled this book in one week. I crafted a 90-page workbook in 3 days. I am a deeply intuitive listener to the point where I can share messages with others from the Universe when they cannot hear it themselves. I can inspire the heck out of people to pursue their purpose. I can see people for the greatness that they are.

Our gifts excite and delight! Follow your passion, and you'll find your gift.

Our Awareness of Our Gifts Evolve Over Time

I coached a Colombian American woman, whose father passed away when she was 9 years old due to an aortic rupture. His aorta burst in this heart within five years of the family immigrating to the U.S.

She had always been deeply interested in medicine. When she would scrape her knee as a little girl, she would dig into the wound even deeper to just to take a look at what was in there. This passion was even greater after she processed her father's death, and she was particularly passionate about practicing medicine in Latino/a communities. Her personal experiences and her community of interest were clear. And even her curiosity about the human body was also clear.

However, the fullness of her gifts hadn't yet revealed themselves to her.

While she did well in her pre-med programs, she was not exercising her gifts. The gift that she had neglected was the human side of health: education, outreach, and advocacy through the process of telling stories. It was when she found public health that she started doing the work that keyed in to her passion. And today, after coaching with me, she has connected the dots even more and reached more nuanced awareness of her gifts through cognitive behavioral work.

Our gift is the piece that we tend to ignore.

Don't just choose the subject area. Like medicine, or economic development, or housing.

Don't just serve the community. Like low-income, minority communities, or LGBT communities.

Take note of your gift. What are the activities, actions, daily experiences that make you come alive? What brings your delight and joy? These are our divine gifts.

> EXERCISE: Make a list of your superpowers. What's your magic touch? What activities bring you delight and joy? What inspires you? How do you inspire others? During what activities are you so engrossed in that you lose track of time?

When we hit the sweet spot of wisdom, community, and divine gifts, that is when we come home to ourselves and experience the richness of living life in Full Color.

> EXERCISE: Break out that journal! Now that you have reflected upon your life experiences, your communities of belonging, and your gifts, reflect on this: what is your purpose this season?

The Great Homecoming: Returning to First Love
Congratulations on going through this journey! So many don't take the time to discover their purpose and calling.

What we might find when going down this rabbit hole is that what we were meant to do, we had loved doing all along.

Today, as Senior Vice President of *CoachDiversity Institute*™, I get to train and facilitate spaces for personal growth, awareness, and social change. And I get to do this work in diverse spaces with leaders of the most amazing and intriguing and refreshing backgrounds.

It turns out that I knew all along that I love facilitating growth and the expansion of human potential in spaces honoring diversity. This is the type of work that I did as a student leader back in high school. Even at that early stage in my life, I was clear about what I loved. There was no need to discover it. It was just a matter of returning home to myself. The truth is we were born in full alignment with who we are. We were born knowing and exploring the things that delight us. We just forgot them.

And just like Dorothy of the *Wizard of Oz*, we can't know or appreciate or enjoy or delight in home, until our experiences have taken us far from home.

So, revel in it all — the discomfort, the struggle, the rejoicing, the home-coming. Revel and delight in it all.

NINE

....

A. is for Alignment

So far, we've worked on strengthening *intuition*, shaping a new *mindset* for success, and discovered our *purpose* and *passion*. Now, for the real fun.

Let's start walking the path and bringing our vision into reality one step at a time. And how we do that is through alignment. Alignment is intentional decision-making whereby you, your life, and all of your resources are all in line with your vision, your purpose, and your passion.

Some of what needs to be in alignment with your dreams include:
- YOU
- mind / thoughts
- emotions
- behaviors
- energy
- body
- physical space
- time
- money
- relationships
- routines

EXERCISE: Willpower check! Before we dive in, take some time to do some journaling. There are about to be some changes. How willing are you to do this work of alignment? What might be holding you back? What do you need to do to prepare yourself for this work?

Developing Your Personal Compass

The time for making decisions based on our fears and external motivations, is over. The time for self-sabotage is over.

Together, let's leverage our internal guidance, let's put our Inner Wisdom to work, letting it determine our direction.

If you want to live life in Full Color and make the impact of a lifetime, you must follow an internal compass. Knowing your values and what drives you is a critical part of that work.

Companies and organizations use their core values to drive decision-making, priorities, direction, and strategy. Similarly, personal values reveal to us as individuals what matters most, and help us make everyday decisions and critical life choices.

Take an Inventory of Your Values

Personal values are the beliefs and principles that make what we do in life worthwhile, meaningful, and important. They are the essence of who we are, at any given moment of our lives. When our values are based on inspiration — as opposed to fear — our values are a strong component of creating a life that we desire. When fear influences our values, we create a limited, less fulfilling life.

Let's look an some examples of how to determine what our core values are. A pastime of mine in a previous stage of life was dance and performance. The reasons why I found dance worthwhile and meaningful came down to the following core values: expression, humanity (the honoring of shared human experience), collaboration, teamwork, inspiring others, excellence, challenge, hard work, and connection.

In my career, I found my work in politics meaningful for the following reasons: justice, community, empowerment, hope, inclusion, leadership, and inspiring others.

At home, as a wife and new mom, family is a top value. I strive to honor the values of teamwork, collaboration, unconditional love, and inspiring others in every aspect of my family life.

Notice that the same values show up in different areas of our lives because the essence of who we are does not change when we move from one area to another. If one area of your life is less than satisfactory, it is likely that you are not honoring one of your top values. Here are some key ways to unveil your top five personal values, and start using your personal compass:

EXERCISE: Brainstorm a list of all the values that are important to you. Take an inventory of your life, past work experiences, relationships, family life, hobbies, and community activities. Think of all the things in which you invest your energy and your time. Notice that there may be multiple reasons why each item is important to you. List all of them out. Distill each reason into a single word or concept. Combine and sort them until you have a great list.

Make Sure Your Values Are Not Fear-Based

If you base decisions in life on fear, it doesn't matter whether you reach your goals or milestones, the fear will still persist, and you will be stuck on the proverbial hamster wheel.

For example, let's take the core value of reputation. Reputation may be important to you because in high school you were not the most popular among your peers, and you are trying to fill an unresolved pain from the past, you might make your decisions to win a popularity contest as an adult. You may make decisions because it looks good from the outside, as opposed to the fact that it would lead to inner fulfillment. Another example may be the value of security. If security is a value because you have lost everything in the past, then it may lead you to stay small. In both these examples, when our values are based on fear and external pressures rather than our dreams and passions, we limit our potential at achieving true inner fulfillment.

Choose Your Top Five Values

After you have your list of personal powerful values, it is important to narrow them down.

Your top five values describe the core essence of who you are in this moment in time. When you look at the top five values that you have selected, you may feel inspired or feel a sense of wholeness. If you don't, what's missing? Make any necessary tweaks. Remember, our values do change over time, so there is no pressure to get this "perfect." I do a values assessment for myself at least once each year.

EXERCISE: Take your list of values that you have brainstormed. Cross-out ones that are not as important to you. Combine the ones that have the same basic meaning to you. For example, being a strong partner, a loving mother, and someone who contributes financially to my family are all important. The single word of "family" captures each of these for me.

Make a Game Plan

This is the real stuff of alignment. It doesn't matter if we know our core values if we don't honor them in our choices and decisions. In creating a game plan based on our present personal values, we are able to live a life of Full Color.

EXERCISE: For each core value, rate yourself on a scale of 1-10, 10 being full integrity, on how well you are honoring your values. In which areas of your life are you walking the talk? In which areas of life are you out of alignment with your values? At home, at work, in your social circle and community life?

For each value, make a game plan to bring your life into greater alignment with that value. Commit to it. This is where the work gets done. For each value, what changes would you like to make that would better align you with that value? By when would you like to make these changes?

Create Your Life With Intention

In 2013, the year after my Awakening, incredible things happened. I married my soul mate, and together we bought a dream home with its very own garden! I started my inspiring coaching business, bringing in more revenue than I thought possible in Year 1. To top it off, I got published in a best-selling compilation. In fact, each year after my Awakening has been the best year of my life.

During my Awakening, I discovered that my life is in my hands – that *I* hold the power to create my own life. When you step into your own power and use your capacity to create your life, awesome things happen! Now, let me share with you this simple yet life-changing process.

Set aside some time for yourself to do this every year, every quarter, or as often as you like. In 2009, I treated myself to a brunch date on New Year's Eve and wrote my intentions on a napkin. Every single one of those intentions came true!

A lot of people think that setting goals are about tangible changes. About landing a big deal, getting a huge promotion or dream job, building that business, finally getting on that healthy diet and losing a few extra pounds, or banking a million for retirement. All of these goals are great, but only if you are intentional about *how* you want to experience those amazing changes in your life.

So next, think about how you will *feel* when doing the things on your list. What *feelings* come to mind? Write these feelings next to each experience on your list.

After you have this core list of feelings, stare at it, soak it all in, speak it aloud. Achieving these feelings *is* the real goal that we are after, not the milestones that we think are goals. How can we live life in a way that makes us *feel* like the phenomenal women we are?

Know that as we evolve and grow, so do our goals and the feelings that come with them.

But while we are here, in this very moment, it is important to be present and experience all those feelings you've identified.

EXERCISE: First, make a list of experiences that you would like to bring into fruition. Let yourself brainstorm and daydream freely. Set aside any judgments about what's possible and what's not. Start small if you'd like. Then go as big as you wish! Write down anything that needs shifting: relationships at work or at home, your finances, your health, your career, anything. What do you want to invite into your life? For each experience, note the core feeling that you wish to embody predominantly from that experience. For example, if the item is to climb Mount Everest, the core feeling might be exhilaration. After you list a core feeling for each item, you will have a list of core feelings that you want to experience in life generally.

Choose your power word. To bring powerful focus for your attention, choose one word out of all your brainstorming that will be your power word for this season.

Create a beautiful inspiring representation of this word.

For those who are visually inspired, break out your magazines, your markers, crayons, and paper. Create a visual work of art, or purchase an inspired piece in the marketplace. Put it somewhere you can see daily.

For those most moved by sound, create a power mixtape of music that inspires you.

For those most inspired by smell, create a blend of spices and herbs that you can return to for peace of mind, or search for an inspiring incense or scented candle that will bring you home to this power word.

There are many ways to create this representation of our power word!

Every time you feel flustered, angry, out of balance, out of whack, or otherwise a bit crunchy, it's a sign that you are out of alignment with your intentions. It's not anyone else's fault. We are in control of our own experience. It's simple. Return to your power word; return to your artistic representation of the word. Return home. Remind yourself of the intention that you are setting. This is your "True North" and your compass.

Finally, share your vision with someone. There is power in verbalizing your vision. Once you speak an intention, it becomes a part of you, and further strengthens your thought process. The simple act of sharing your intentions with a loved one is enough to get the ball rolling. The more you share your intentions, the more support you beckon and receive to make them a reality.

One of my core words for the past few years has been POWER. I will stand in all of my power to create and make change in this world as I know I am called to.

So, discover your power word and share your intention. I know with 100 percent certainty that by doing this, you can create a life you love. You deserve it. We deserve the REAL you too! And the world needs the real you.

Clear the Clutter

In order to bring in the new, we must make space. Out with the old, in with the new! Just like skin, we need to shed old, dull surface cells to reveal the fresh glow that lies beneath!

To make space, simplify your life. Get things off your plate and focus on your priorities. Let go of pressure and stress you don't need or want. Strip your focus down to the basics. Determine your own top priorities and focus on one thing at a time. You can do it! And it doesn't have to be complicated. Life is as complicated or as simple as we make it.

There are many kinds of clutter that we need to clear — physical, emotional, spiritual, and bodily clutter, relational clutter, paper clutter, digital clutter, temporal clutter, just to name a few.

EXERCISE: For each type of clutter (physical, emotional, spiritual, and bodily clutter, relational clutter, paper clutter, digital clutter, temporal clutter), make lists of what you are ready, willing, and able to let go.

Take a look at this list. What emotions, if any, come up when you think about clearing this clutter? What might be keeping you from clearing the clutter? What does this clutter signify to you? Who would you be without the clutter?

After this reflection, create an action plan. What steps will you take to clear the clutter?

Many of us have challenges clearing our clutter, because doing so represents change. If you need help, get help from friends, family, support groups, or other professionals, like coaches and consultants. Do reading to help shift your mindset around your clutter.

We have already talked about clearing a lot of mental and emotional clutter when we discussed our mindset. Now, let's take a look at another valuable resource: our time.

Reclaim Your Time

Time management is a critical piece of getting intentional about our lives and creating the experience we want. It means getting really honest about what we want and don't want. It means making tough decisions and saying no, even if it might mean hurting others. We can't please everyone, and if we try, we will run ourselves down.

When you are feeling like time is getting away from you, do some reflection around your commitments. About which commitments are you 100 percent passionate? Which commitments are starting to feel like a chore? Which commitments do you approach as a bore? Which commitments overwhelm you? To love and respect ourselves unconditionally means to love and respect our schedules as well. To stay true to this goal, we have to take a real hard look at how we spend our time.

Learn to Say "No"

After my Awakening, I started volunteering at the community art space as the director of the art gallery. After the successful and warm community art show, and after my 30th birthday celebration there, I started having second thoughts about how much time I actually had to commit to the space. It was a space that I loved and believed in, but when I sat down to write the Truth, the Truth was that I did not want to be the gallery director. The Truth was that I was nervous about committing to the space because it needs a lot of love and care, and that I needed to give that love and care to myself.

I got honest. I wrote to the head of the art gallery to let him know that I could only commit to direct the gallery through the end of that month, and that I needed to re-focus my time on my new priorities. I didn't like backing out of commitments. I did not want to be flaky. To me, that meant that people would not be able to rely on me when I had built up an expectation. But, by this time, I loved myself more than overcommitting my time to something I was not 100 percent passionate. Even though I felt tinges of guilt, I moved forward anyway. It was time to let go of guilt and pleasing others to meet outside pressures. It was time to create more space for myself and my own priorities. It was a new era to reclaim my time. At the end of the day, he was sad to see me go, but definitely understood.

Another activity I had picked up was dancing. After a few months of it, I started to get overwhelmed with the level of expectation and commitment that my dance teacher wanted. This teacher was in the process of building a dance company, and he expected the highest level of commitment from his dancers. One day, I took a class with a female teacher, one with less expectation and pressure, and it was lovely. It was for me – it felt relaxed and easy. Rather than a rehearsal with high expectations, it was a celebration of womanhood. Once again, I had the opportunity to develop my practice of saying "no." Once again, it was disappointing to my teacher, but I had to develop this muscle of making room for myself if I was to regain sanity.

A theme was emerging. I was getting turned off by commitments when expectations were high, and when they were not in sync with the self-love, space, and easiness that I needed particularly during that period of my life. So much of my life had been about meeting other people's expectations as opposed to pursuing what made me happy.

Despite my love of art and dance, I had to dig deep in my soul to connect more with what I wanted – to fulfill these passions of mine on *my own* terms.

To do this, I needed to learn how to say no to these commitments in order to de-clutter and make space and time to pursue what would fulfill me. It is like a muscle: the more we practice, the stronger we get. So, the more we de-clutter, the more we can pursue our own passions. The more we honor our own priorities and values, the more easily we can express ourselves authentically.

EXERCISE: Get clear about your own priorities and what is important to you. Make an inventory of your commitments and time-sucks. Which commitments would you like to take off your plate? Clear off your plate and off your schedule everything that is extraneous. Do some commitments take longer than they need to? Cut them short! You have the power!

What Keeps Us From Clearing Our Schedules

Learning to say "no," clearing your calendar, and drawing boundaries are integral pieces to cultivating sanity and fulfillment. Here are five common excuses and reasons that people give for not being able to clear their schedules. Let's bust through them!

#1: I will disappoint people if I step away.

One thing that might keep you from saying no or drawing boundaries is your fear of letting others down. Here's the scoop. Of course, people might be disappointed, hurt, and sad to see you go! I stepped down from being CEO at the Asian Pacific American Institute for Congressional Studies, and board members have told me they were sad, upset, mad, and disappointed with me. Two and a half years after I left, one board member told me he was still upset with me! After seeing a picture of my son, and understanding that my priorities have changed, he finally came around and said, "oh alright, I forgive you."

If we pack our schedules with commitments just to please other people, we are strengthening our practice of living for others. And before we know it, we have undone all our progress to live in accordance with our own values and priorities, and are back where we started: feeling incredible stress and pressure because we've handed over our power to others.

#2: No one else can do it like I do it!

Perhaps perfectionist tendencies may make it difficult to let go and move on from certain responsibilities like leading big projects at work, board commitments, community service roles, or household responsibilities.

Get over it!

For example, I am always eager to split the time spent caring for our child with my husband. One weekend, he finally did relieve me of the responsibility of putting our son down for his afternoon nap. When he was doing it, I noticed that I was judging him every step of the way for not doing it exactly as I would have! After 15 minutes of pure frustration, I had to leave the house to actually enjoy my time alone, and just let it go.

#3: I am giving up a part of myself.

Sometimes, we feel reluctant to "give up" the part of ourselves that the particular commitment may represent for us.

For the multi-passionate, it's okay to say no. Trust that you can always get back to this particular passions later. Stepping down from my post as a volunteer art gallery director, and leaving an informal dance company led by my friend, did not mean I was leaving art for good – I was just putting them on the back-burner for a bit. I was making space to breathe and to live without pressure. Both activities and commitments meant a great deal to me. My love for the arts is, and always will be, an integral part of who I am. However, when I was getting honest with myself, both commitments caused me more stress than joy. It was time to let them go. Years later, I got back to the arts through impromptu dance classes, picking up water-color painting, and signing up for a vocal performance at a nonprofit fundraising event.

Remember, letting go of an activity does NOT mean losing a part of your identity. Our identities are shaped and molded over time. We are not static beings! It is okay to let go.

#4: Asking for help is weak.

Remember, thoughts lead to emotions lead to action. If I believe that asking for help is weak, I will feel shame for needing it. Then I will not ask for help, and I will get burnt out.

What new perception is possible? What else can assistance represent besides weakness? It can mean providing the opportunity for others to grow and develop. It can mean generosity.

When it comes to family, community, or work responsibilities, by stepping aside, stepping down, and asking for help, we are doing everyone a great service! Others may be happy and willing to help, and even excited for the opportunity. When we let go, we make room to for others to be themselves, cultivate their own powers, and become future leaders too! Amazing!

Asking for and needing help is a normal part of living in community. It is participating in the natural ebb and flow of things. I love helping, and I know others love helping as well. By creating new perceptions around help, I am able to feel good about shifting things off my plate by asking for help. In doing this, I expand my potential and the potential of all those around me.

Is there someone else who is fit and positioned to do this task? Then delegate! Oftentimes multi-talented leaders take on many leadership positions or responsibilities and may put undue pressure on themselves to continue carrying the burden. Perhaps perfectionist tendencies make it difficult to let go and move on. Perhaps we may feel shame because we think that we are giving up or letting others down. We may not realize that stepping aside, stepping down, and asking for help will develop future leaders, and others may be happy and willing to step up to the plate.

#5: Prioritizing myself is self-centered.

Many of us may come from cultural backgrounds, families, and communities where prioritizing ourselves is not an accepted practice and considered self-centered.

First, remember that culture ebbs and flows. Culture evolves based on the people who live and move through it, and create it. We are living and breathing beings. Culture is not static. It changes and always has.

Second, I affirm that putting myself is indeed self-centered: I am becoming centered in my self. And I love that. To put it another way, if I run myself down, then my spirit also becomes weak. In this state, I am of no use to my family, loved ones, and certainly am of diminishing use to my community. Show me a leader who is not centered in their own selves, and I'll show you someone on their way to burn out (or already there).

It all boils down to self-love. The moment that I learned to love myself for who I am, and the moment that I acknowledged that I have a unique role to play in the world and in my community, the happier I became, the more trust I had, the more capacity I had to serve, and the more passionate I became about service. If anyone tells me that loving myself is not "Chinese" or not "Asian" or goes against my family, I'm happy to let their comment go with confidence and trust in who I am. At the end of the day, my life is my life. I do what works for me, and what is meaningful for me.

When I care for my self, I invite care into my life
and I care for the other. When I care for the other,
I care for my self. It is all the same.
– The Buddha

135

Remember, being centered in your self IS the greatest service and gift that you can provide to the rest of us.

Structure Gives Way to Freedom

Now that we have busted through common excuses that keep people from de-cluttering their schedules, let's talk about creative ways to proactively manage our time.

First, train yourself to set scheduling parameters. Set boundaries, or for the freedom-lovers, a loose framework for your schedule. Block off sections of time where you will only focus on certain priorities, certain types of meetings, certain commitments. Place these time blocks on your calendar and then stick to them!

Let your friends, family, and associates know about this so they understand and support your commitments. By creating structure and boundaries around time you will find freedom – freedom to reach your top goals and intentions within the parameters you have set for yourself.

For example, I have assigned particular days of each week that are dedicated to client calls, in-person meetings, and marketing. I handle all of my scheduling accordingly.

Some clients say they will network three times a week, dedicate one day or evening a week to time with friends and families, and then devote a certain evening or day of the week to personal time.

Structure gives way to freedom. And remember: be kind to yourself. You can always tweak the parameters if they do not work for you. Don't give up on them!

Think of Creative Solutions.

With a new positive mindset, focus and direction, and greater freedom, it's easy to come up with creative ways to tweak the demands on your time. Structure your creative solutions in a way that honors your values.

Do you want to make time for both socializing with friends and exercise? Grab a running buddy or go on a bike ride for your social time! Need to have food at home for the kids, but have to work late? Let a thermal cooker or a slow-cooker do the work for you! I used to think that weekends must be set aside for quality time with the husband, but turns out that he likes certain time slots to take afternoon naps. This used to drive me nuts because I felt like I was wasting precious time, but now, I see this as an opportunity for me to get out of the house and do some networking, yoga class, or grocery-shopping.

Take Back Control! Set Your Own Rhythm.

Take time to create the life that you want. Think through the daily, weekly, monthly, annual, and the life rhythm that you want. What are the key things that you want to experience this cycle? Know yourself, know your direction.

When we feel overwhelmed by issues around time, it's because what is on our schedules and how we spend our time is not aligned with our priorities, our values, and what we want our life to look like. When we take control over the direction and priorities in our lives, that's when we have a strong compass that will help guide us to say yes, no, or help! Ask yourself: by the end of this quarter or this year, what three things would I like to accomplish?

And importantly, ask yourself, why? What is my definition of success for this time period? When you ask yourself why, you unveil your true motivations and drivers. All the "have-to's" and "should's" on our lists become "want-to's." We become more excited and engaged, and less stressed and overwhelmed.

Bottom line is: don't fight with your schedule. Instead, make your schedule work for you!

The Myth About Having It All

As we plan our lives, there is a myth out there circulating about "Having it All" that I would like to dispel once and for all! There are so many well-meaning experts out there saying "you can't have it all!" or "work-life balance doesn't exist."

Anytime someone tells you that you CAN'T do something, plug up your ears and turn the other way.

They are eroding your belief in, and therefore, your ability to focus and concentrate on achieving your dreams.

I'm about to tell you the secret to having it all. Here goes.

The problem with how most people talk about "having it all," is the false premise that "all" means the same thing to all people. When experts say you can't "have it all," they are likely talking about being a White, upper-middle-class woman, and balancing a high-powered career while raising a family with two young children and a husband who also has a high-powered career.

Here's the false premise: that the above is what we all want. This is a premise that some of us don't even question for ourselves. We may think we want it because we have been programmed to believe that it is the "all" that we should all strive for. We've been conditioned to believe that this particular "all" *is* success itself, forgetting that we get to define what success looks like for ourselves.

Define for yourself what "having it all" means for you.

For me, all the work that I do to step into my own power is not worth a dime if I fail to maintain balance in my home life and in my relationships with my loved ones.

As I build my two businesses and manage a household, every so often my husband and I get into conflict. One time, he brought to my attention that when he would talk, I literally would not hear him and would not respond. It's as if I had a husband filter, and everything coming in was not even registering.

The second time he brought it up to me, I was so angry and frustrated, not with the fact that my husband wasn't feeling heard, but that I didn't even notice what I was doing, that part of me didn't want to change, and that I felt tremendous guilt that I could devote 100 percent of my undivided attention to my business, my husband, or my child. I felt resentful! After all, that argument in particular was about something as mundane as putting raspberries in our son's oatmeal. My perspective at the time was that I could not handle fighting over little things like oatmeal!

After some prayer and meditation time, I kept getting the same message over and over. Wife. Mom. Boss. In that order. Wife. Mom. Boss. This meant that my anger was misdirected at my husband. What I was really angry about was that my life was out of alignment with my core values, my desires, and what really mattered to me. Now I am working on ways to balance Marriage. Son. Business. In that order. To have these three priorities in balance is my "having it all."

For me, a happy home life is one of my deepest desires. If I had a thriving business, but my marriage was up in flames, or my son felt neglected, would it be worth it? Absolutely NOT.

In order to walk my talk, I must make sure that my everyday decisions reflect a reverence to this desire. If I prioritize too much of my to-do list in my business over spending quality family time, in the long-term, I will not "have it all" as I define it.

For example, one decision that I had to make was more quality time with family. I recently decided that it is more important to me that our household has family fun days on Sundays than for this book to be published on a more expedited schedule. I can still have a strong family and be a published author. I can have it all on my own time, on my own terms, and in my own balanced way.

Last but certainly not least is self-care. If I strive to meet "all" the demands of my business and family, but fall apart myself, I am no use to anyone at all.

So, as I fine-tune what "having it all" means to me, I continue to eternally adjust the balance between work, life, and self-care that I desire. I can truly shape my life based on my own desires. I can get intentional about which priorities are most important and most urgent. I can let go of things that do not matter in the long-run.

We have to give ourselves space to figure out this balance as life unfolds. We *can* have it all, but we must continually define what "all" means for us. Everyone's ranking of priorities will not be the same. And even if you have the same priorities as someone else, you may not rank them in the same order.

Make sure you make time to discover and understand your own priorities. How do you choose?

AFFIRM:

I am balance.

I am ease.

I am worthy of balance and ease.

EXERCISE: Create a list of your top priorities. Ask yourself questions about their importance in your life and how each priority impacts the other. Will the urgency of this particular matter make a difference 1 year from now? 5 years? 10 years? Force yourself to ask these hard questions, and rank your priorities. After you make a list in priority order, what needs to change in your life to match your prioritization? Clarity will follow.

Finally, what does self-care mean for you? In what ways will you honor self-care? Every week? Every month? Every year?

Quit Old Habits; Become the New You

Finally, let's talk about quitting habits for which we no longer have a use and adopting empowering ones. Resolutions and goals — the kind you cherish — are not about restricting your behavior, restraining yourself, or telling yourself no – you can't eat this or you can't do that. It's also not about telling yourself that you "should" be doing something. When you "should" yourself, you are shaming yourself. And shame is definitely not something we want to increase in our lives! Think of when you are working with a child. When you tell a small child that they can't do something or that they must do something, what happens? The child doesn't listen, or does so begrudgingly, and perhaps builds up a shame reservoir for wanting something different.

Your soul is the same way. You either fuel it or you smother it. If you tell it no, it's not going to listen. If you tell it that it "should", it will not understand. You've gotta say YES to something new.

I really love saying YES! And there's a reason why joyful people say yes. It's because saying yes floods our bodies with hormones that makes us feel good. And, I don't mean saying yes as in over-committing or people-pleasing. Remember: it is about saying yes to ourselves, practicing self-love and being centered in ourselves.

Life starts to shift tremendously when we start saying yes to what we want, where we are on our journeys, and what we are grateful for – the good stuff and the challenges. When we say YES, we train ourselves to become grateful for difficulties that lead to growth and learning. We sharpen our ability to look for the opportunities in all that is before us. We become nimble, adaptive, and accepting of challenges as experiences to delight us. We become grateful for the situations in front of us as opportunities for learning, even those that cause us discomfort.

It's not enough to stream half-baked positive thoughts through your mind, and expect your life to change! You have to really mean it and feel it! Say it aloud and move your body. Give voice and physical vibration to your YES! You have to feel it deeply, and believe it — consistently over time — for it to transform your life. This is the only way that you can authentically impact your own life and those around you.

Rather than saying "no" to the old, say "Yes!" and embrace change. Get SUPER excited! Have FUN!

BECOME the new YOU.
I used to be a smoker. There was a time in my twenties when I tried to quit because a guy I was trying to impress thought smoking was gross. Needless to say, a few weeks later I picked up those nasty butts again.

2011 was the year that I was finally able to quit. How? It was no longer about what I "should" or "shouldn't" do. It wasn't about pleasing someone else. It was about pleasing me. It was about becoming the person I chose to BE. And that new person had different thoughts, different focus, and a new outlook on life. Remember Albert Einstein's definition of insanity: "Doing the same thing over and over again, and expecting different results." If you think the same old thoughts, that old habit will be just as difficult to quit as the last time you tried.

I didn't become a non-smoker that year — I became a woman who loved herself and every single cell of her body. This included my lungs, and my vocal chords. It wasn't about shame. It was about love. It was about air. It was about breath. It was about life itself!

In 2011, I was a woman who wanted to express her true self, and there was no other option but to say "Yes!" My soul was 100 percent behind my decision, and all of a sudden, quitting became easy and fun. To support myself, the week I quit, I signed up for voice lessons, something I always wanted to do. I enjoyed every minute of it, and when I found out the tunes that could come out of my body, I quickly forgot about nicotine.

EXERCISE: Grab your journal! Here we go!

1. What's the resolution? Ask yourself, what's the habit you think you "should" quit, or the one you "should" take on?

2. Get to the bottom of it. WHY do you really want it so much? What values are behind this desire? List them all out. There are lots of reasons for quitting: health, vitality, strength, energy, love. So what's your top value? Choose one. After you choose it, make sure it is a noun.

3. Become that value. Add an "I AM" in front of it to superpower your intention. Then change your thoughts and actions to align with the value, one at a time. For me, my mantra that year was "I am self-love." That year, you bet I BECAME self-love, and not just by quitting some habit.

4. Don't beat yourself up. This will prevent you from becoming this value – the new you. Congratulate yourself for coming this far. And try again. It's always another brand new day!

5. Finally, make it fun! List out all the super fun ways that you could support yourself in becoming this value. Do one thing on that list.

Remember: It's always about who <u>you</u> want to be.

Starting today, you get to choose. Who will you decide to BE starting right now?

TEN

....

C. is for Courage

The "C" in the I.M.P.A.C.T. Principle™ stands for *Courage*. The Merriam-Webster dictionary defines it as the: "mental or moral strength to venture, persevere, and withstand danger, fear, or difficulty." Courage is critical to sustaining the momentum for living a fulfilling life in Full Color. Why? Because living in Full Color means constantly reinventing ourselves anew. This is brave work.

Let's dive in.

They Didn't Risk It All for Me to Play it Safe

My parents jumped into unknown waters in the dark of night. Dreams. Freedom. A sense of self they had never known. A reason to live. This motivated my dad to swim seven hours across the Deep Bay from Communist China to freedom in Hong Kong. That's what pushed my mom to swim across tightly patrolled Shen Zhen River, with more dogs, guards, and guns.

My parents grew up during the Cultural Revolution without much of a childhood. When my father was nine, his own father was imprisoned in a labor camp. After that time, my father very rarely saw his own father. My parents were deprived of their high school education and sent to reeducation camps for hard farm labor. Their lives were fraught with family separation, political persecution, and constant surveillance. I wonder which was more difficult: backbreaking labor or the psychological trauma of constantly having to prove themselves revolutionary and pure.

Growing up, every time I faced a challenge and shared my feelings about it, my mother always scolded me. "We crawled out from Hell and survived! What you're going through, this is nothing."

Her remarks never made me feel better. Instead, I felt invisible and small; cowering in the shadows of the tremendous suffering my parents had endured.

After immigrating to New York in their late twenties, they started as factory workers — my father in a noodle factory and my mother in a garment factory. They worked hard to support us little ones, all the while stumbling over new words and strange phrases, and attending school to earn their higher education. My father worked long hours at the factory during the day and went to school in the evenings. After my father earned his degree, it was my mother's turn. She would attend classes during the weekdays and work as a secretary at the music school that my sister and I attended. This allowed her to juggle earning an income and keeping an eye over us on the weekends. After many years of this hectic life, my father eventually became an executive at the noodle company, and my mother became an esteemed ethnic journalist, and is now a published author.

My story is born from theirs. My courage begins with theirs.

While in my twenties, I felt the guilt and pressure of never being enough to make up for their sacrifices. Today, I understand that they did not risk it all for me to play it safe. I am also coming to fully understand why it is that they support and love me as much as they do.

I am moved by my parents' tremendous courage. From their courage I am able to channel that same beautiful fearlessness to create my own life.

In spite of our fear, let's jump into these unknown waters, and swim in it. Swim in it, not just for survival, but also for joy.

I asked my dad about his seven-hour swim:

> "Weren't you scared?"

> "Of course."

> "How did you make it?" I asked.

> "There was nothing else to do but swim."

The First Small Step: Have Faith and Walk Into Your Fears

All of this work takes courage because we are headed into the unknown. In the beginning, pursuing our dreams to make our visions a reality may feel uncomfortable. This is normal. We are entering new territory, pushing boundaries, and overcoming fears. We are transitioning.

Rest assured, you are not a coward. Fear is a normal part of the process. You are conquering fear. You are growing.

Bringing our vision into the world takes courage because it requires fundamental shifts in identity. Our egos are attached to the known, and to our previous, sometimes deeply engrained, sense of self. We must believe bigger. Our view of ourselves must expand, and we must believe bigger.

The fear all makes sense. And guess what? To live a life of freedom, purpose, and delight – the life you are meant to live – you must first walk *through* the fear to get past it. In fact, we continuously move through fear as we continue our never-ending journey of growth.

Say, "Yes!" and take the next step forward. Walk toward fear!

We have to trust and hold fast to our inspired vision. We don't have to know every detail to take that first step.

> *Faith is taking the first step*
> *even when you don't see the whole staircase.*
> *- Dr. Martin Luther King, Jr.*

Have faith and take that first step. Keep climbing the staircase. Begin to walk through your fears. Let yourself dream. Begin to get clear. Join forces with the Universe and own your role as co-creator of your life. As you step through your fears, things will start to become clearer and clearer, and – I promise – easier and easier.

You are in for a wild ride.

To Walk Through Our Fears, We Must Know Our Fears.

In order to make courageous choices in the direction of our dreams, we need to discern which decisions we are making based on fears and which we are making based on our dreams and visions. We want to shift from allowing our fears to control our decisions and tap into the subconscious to make our dreams come alive!

Get clear. What is the courageous decision that you want to make? Is it a new job? Starting a new business? Meeting a new partner? Releasing an old partner? Telling the truth? Using your voice? Speaking? Leading?

Remember, you are the only expert in whether it is the right time to make a courageous decision to change something in your life. Nobody can tell you when the right time is to walk through fear. You hold the reigns. You will know when the time is right.

EXERCISE: At the top of a blank page, write out the change that you are contemplating. Next, brainstorm all the reasons preventing you from making this change. List them all out.

Next, make a two-column table. At the top of one column, write the word "EXCUSE" and at the top of the other column write the word "CHOICE."

Sort into the two columns all of the reasons you listed that are preventing you from making your change.

Explore each item. If you poke holes at it, does it hold water? If the reasoning falls apart, then place it in the EXCUSE column.

However, if that reason is based truly on a preference of how you wish to create in your ideal life, then it is a choice. If it is based on the way in which you want to bring your vision into the world, then move it to the CHOICE column.

Connect with your Inner Wisdom to discern between the two.

Finally, for each item in the EXCUSE pile, decide whether or not you need to make a contingency plan or shore up your strengths and leverage your resources so that feel confident moving forward. Create an action plan to wipe out that excuse once and for all.

For example, one of my clients was very passionate about wellness and leadership in the workplace. She dreamed of creating a business around these issues.

However, as we worked together, it came up that she was doing informational interviews for full-time positions. Screeeecchhh! Hold up! What happened? I thought she wanted her own business.

After some probing, she started naming reasons why she couldn't go for her big dream of starting her own business. As we went through each reason, one by one, she sorted through which were excuses, which were choices, and which were not yet clear. Remember, there are no right answers.

Reason #1: She did not have any official title or position in providing wellness and leadership services. She felt she lacked the experience and expertise to deliver services with excellence. However, I knew that she had plenty of experience training and providing workshops around these topics. I asked her, "If I were a company representative that wanted to hire you for support in the areas of leadership and wellness, what services would you be able to provide?" Of course her answer showed all of her expertise and readiness to work. So, her initial reason of lacking experience and expertise was an EXCUSE. She had all the experience and expertise necessary to perform her services.

Reason #2: As an entrepreneur, she wouldn't have the benefit of organizational support with experts and advisors. I asked: "If you could build your business and seek advisors and mentors to help you, would you still prefer to have the support of an organizational structure?" Her answer was, "no." So that one was an EXCUSE. Sometimes, when we discover and excuse, it is an opportunity to make a plan! If she were ready to move forward in the business, the next step for her would be to ask herself: What guidance and mentorship would I like along the way?

Reason #3: As an entrepreneur, she wouldn't have the security of steady income from a 9-5 job. Here was her thought process: Her household has current financial needs. In business, it takes time to build a sustainable business with monthly steady cashflow. It takes time. She decided that what she really wanted was to choose to apply for a 9-5 to meet her household's financial needs, while she builds her business on the side. So this final reason of meeting household financial obligations, she placed in the CHOICE column.

Through this exercise, we gain clarity. We do gut checks to make sure we are not driven by fear. We make plans so that we make our courageous transitions work for us. We allow things to unfold on their own time without forcing the issue or shaming ourselves.

Remember there is no right or wrong answer. There is no judgment. This is all part of your journey. Take the time to discover your fears so you can embrace your gifts and your vision. When you are ready, you will be able to let go and move through these fears, and into your vision.

What About the Money?

Money is one area that can really hold us back. Over and over, I hear the money excuse. This one might feel like a real hurdle, but like anything else, it is as real or as difficult as we make it in our minds.

Our perceptions of financial barriers are shaped by what we believe is possible.

A friend of mine had a yearning to leave the government to follow his dream. In his mind, it was money that was holding him back from pursuing his passion. Yet he had enough cash to cover a year and a half of expenses. Someone else with a different mindset might jump ship that very moment. For him, a-year-and-a-half cushion was not enough money to overcome this fear.

A Romanian woman that I know always lives life on the edge. She never knows where she will be living the next month, how her immigration papers will be renewed, or how her rent check will be paid. Any single one of these things might wreak havoc on others, but she thrived. She is the most passionate person I've ever met. She loves the thrill of being on the edge. Her gift is living outside the comfort zone. In fact, if she finds herself too comfortable, she creates new challenges for herself. I would listen to her and just revel at how she lived passionately on the edge – without doubt or fear. She lives in pure rapture.

In the end, we each have to make the call as to how much of a safety net we want. We are only human. It is okay to want safety nets. The question is how much do you need?

End the excuses. You can be as fearless or cowardly as you wish when it comes to money. At some point, you jump or you don't. If finances are getting in your way, pick a number. What is the number you need in your bank account for you to be ready to jump? Once you have saved that amount, jump!

Think about it: Do you want to live a life without joy, without pursing your dreams? Or do you want to take a risk, wade through the fear and find bliss?

Strengthen Your Money Mojo

Ok, so you want to stop making the excuses. You ask, but Gloria, show me the money! If your bank account is not where you want it, guess who is responsible? YOU ARE! Even at the time of this writing, I am still open to developing more money mojo! This is one of the great challenges of our time! Let's see what we can do about it.

Check your beliefs about Money. Do you believe money is dirty? Do you believe that in order to earn money that you must work hard? Is your identity tied to the concept that you struggle or that your community struggles? If these are fundamental beliefs for you then you are putting a limit on your financial abundance. These limiting beliefs about money are deeply-rooted in fears associated with money, success, and personal worth. Until you overcome this limiting belief, this fear, you will continue to wonder why it's so hard to make ends meet. You will not be comfortable with the notion of money, and continue to limit your earning and wealth-building potential.

Let's drop the excuses. We all have had limiting beliefs around money. We learn it from our parents, our family history, and our community history. However, it doesn't matter where our beliefs came from. We get to choose our future for ourselves, our families, and our communities. We hold the power.

So let's dive in.

<u>Money is dirty</u>
Recently, I was working on my money mojo. One of the biggest insights around money happened when I found myself doing something that I hardly ever do: I was holding a big, fat wad of cold, hard cash. And it hit me like a firestorm. Bam! The very first thing that came to mind when I held that money was that it was DIRTY. That it was covered in germs and bacteria. The money was literally dirty. My visceral reaction was to wash my hands immediately, or else I would spread disease. Whoa! If that was my response to actual money, no wonder my relationship with money was tentative. There are other things that I encounter in my life that carry germs, like for instance, my son. But DIRTY is not the first thing I think of when I hold my dear boy.

So, what makes money any different? Why was my reaction to money so different than to my son? They are both important in my life and provide me with joy and fulfillment.

How was I going to get past this fear of money? I needed to redefine my relationship with money. What I did for a whole week was carry a fat wad of cash with me. I counted that fat wad joyfully every day to start reforming my relationship with money. I counted it, smelled it, held it in my hands, looked at it, expressed gratitude to the Universe for it, and was excited for more of it. I was appreciative of all the money that every came to me throughout my life. I looked around my house and just rejoiced at the great abundance, as opposed to feeling fear and lack.

I'm not deserving

Here's another example: in my full-time gigs, I never made more than $100,000. While others set goals and milestones for their earnings, I limited my wealth set-point. I capped myself at $100,000 and thus, never made more than that. From where did this come? Why did I create this limit? I dug deep and thought about my life experiences and upbringing.

When I was a young child, my father had never earned more than this sum. He was my role model, caring for our entire family of four on much less. Who was I to make more? After all, in my mind, making six figures meant outpacing my father, and I didn't think I was big enough for that.

This is flawed thinking. As my role model, he wants me to help support my family and be successful. Additionally, my dad continues to be wildly successful today. Plus, as my husband pointed out to me, I had not considered inflation. This changed everything. Recognizing my personal history with money allowed me to change my attitude towards it, and move beyond the limiting beliefs I held about it.

Money is Evil

Another belief is that money is evil, or that if you have wealth, you might be out of touch with people that don't have it. This one is easy to combat. I know given my background and values, that money cannot change me.

Yes, there are many fundamental injustices about our current financial system. However, we have more agency than we know and hold tremendous power to re-define our relationship with money, and define our relationships with one another within this financial system. This is how new systems come into place.

As we move into new ways of interacting with money through entrepreneurship, relationship-building, socially conscious investing, contributing to causes, cultivating entrepreneurship and positive relationships with money in others, we can move powerfully in this system in a way that is aligned with who we are.

Money itself is not evil. It is our relationship with money that can be misaligned with our values. Money is just like everything else. We can be addicted to money or we can have a healthy relationship with it. We can be addicted in our intimate relationships with people or we can have a healthy relationship with them. We can be addicted to our work, or we can have a healthy relationship in our work life.

This is what Spirit / All-That-Is spoke to me one day:

> *I love you. Don't forget! My love will show up in many many ways. Money is just one of them. So, as with any relationship, build your relationship through your Trust in ME, and the relationship will flourish. Try to control the relationship or money, and you're slipping away from me, forgetting me.*
>
> *KEEP ME in the relationship.*
>
> *Love you. xoxo*
>
> *BIG HUGS!!!!*

Money, like anything else, is an avenue through which we experience life. So if you came upon a LOT of money, you don't necessarily become evil.

Let's do a thought experiment to prove it.

> EXERCISE: If you won US$1 billion in lottery winnings, what would you do with the money?

When the Powerball exceeded $900 million (yes, that is 9 with 8 zeroes after it: $900,000,000) my husband was buying tickets in the hopes of winning this enormous sum. So, for fun, I decided to sit down and chart out what we would do with that money. Well, here was my breakdown:

- $600,000,000 would go toward changing the landscape of green technology. We would invest in all the green technologies leaving no excuses for why the US is still lagging behind with old energy issues.
- $200,000,000 would go toward setting up my husband's dream job: running a family foundation to make a social impact in the world.
- $20,000,000 would go to family and friends
- $5,000,000 would go towards the growth of *CoachDiversity Institute*™.
- $2,000,000 would go toward building a retreat center for leadership and holistic events, and
- the rest would go toward taxes and investing in life experiences.

What changes is our potential for impact! When we expand our money mindset and beef up our money mojo, we have a new outlook on money and are able to seek greater opportunities for ourselves, our families, and our communities. Thus, shifting our attitude about money does not change us. It simply changes our capacity for change!

Your relationship with money is only a struggle if you make it one. So, how can you shift your money mindset and beef up your money mojo to create new beliefs about money, your power, and your potential for impact?

EXERCISE: Write a letter to Money. Share your gratitude for how it has supported you throughout your life. Share your feelings toward it, including any fear and doubt. Share your hopes and dreams for your future relationship with Money. What do you want to change? Declare it! Negotiate your relationship with Money. Ask it for any help you need.

As you write your letter, what resistance if any is coming up for you? What emotions are surfacing, if any?

The Awesome Adventure
Accept uncertainty for what it truly is: an awesome adventure.

If you had shown me as a teen how all of this tumultuous yet delicious, beautiful, and inspired life would unfold that would take away all the fun in my personal adventure! If God were to show me right now how every moment of my life is to play out, I might go blind. The Universe never gives us more than we can handle, and every experience is meant to propel us to the next phase of growth.

Not knowing is a part of normal daily human existence. You can either choose to be overwhelmed and stressed out by the unknown, or you can breathe it in and enjoy the ride. Change your perspective and see life for the amazing adventure it is.

Remember what pure childlike wonder felt like? Tap into that wonder and amazement by trusting your deliciously unfolding life. Then experience the delight and surprise of the unknown. Do it daily. Make it a part of your routine.

Positive Expectation

While it is all well and good to set goals and intentions, and keep faith in our visions, sometimes the Universe knows our deepest desires more than we do.

At the end of my first day of my coach certification class, I declared to my husband, I will be the first Asian American coaching trainer at this school! And I was. After I received my coaching certification, I was quickly put on a path to becoming a coach certification trainer. Things happened very quickly and it was a great experience. I was gaining confidence as a teacher and loved the process of helping others learn the awesome trade of coaching. However, the Universe had me in limbo for over a year. As a trainer-in-training I was not getting paid for my services as a trainer. Nothing was happening in the financial front, and there was literally no end in sight.

Meanwhile, every single time I was training, all the stories that I would tell would be about racial or ethnic diversity.

The Universe was preparing me for something more delicious than I could have known. It was preparing me for *CoachDiversity Institute*™. *CoachDiversity Institute*™ was not something I had planned. It was born out of a "chance" encounter between Dr. Towanna Freeman and myself. Dr. Freeman shared with me her vision, and immediately, I knew that I was meant to be a part of this vision. This was an answer to the prayers I never knew I made. The Universe knew my subconscious desires, and had bigger plans for me.

When the time came and we prepared ourselves in full faith and ready to serve, opportunities flowed our way quickly and steadily. Stay ready, stay open, and let go.

We don't always know the complete journey. But the Universe always knows. And when we are open, when we know ourselves and our desires, the Universe always provides. Stay grounded. Stay uplifted. Stay expectant. Stay optimistic.

This unbridled, expansive optimism is incredibly vulnerable. Having big faith is incredibly vulnerable. It is putting our trust and the fulfillment of our deepest desires in the Unseen. It is moving forward on faith without yet having proof. However, it is only with this courage and vulnerability that we are able to tap into our full potential. It is only with this big faith that we deliver big impact with grace.

When we are in this state of positive knowing and trusting that the Universe has our back, that is when it most powerfully shows us the way.

Trust in the process and allow creativity to flow through and drive you. Allow your intuition to lead you to the next path in your journey. Whether it is a baby step or a giant leap, take it. Trust in the Universe. The Universe is within you. You are the Universe.

It's Harvest Time!
You've done all the hard work. You've courageously taken steps, made plans, created partnerships and collaborations. You have invested in new mindset and big faith. It is harvest time.

Enjoy the ride. It is an amazing one...

HARVEST TIME

It's Harvest Time!
It's Harvest Time!

Harvest Time is a favorite time.

The human mind
once awakened
all it wants to do is co-create.
wait
be silent
be still

I chose my own mind to be
the Land where I work

to loosen the soil
clear those weeds
so stubborn
they grip on
grow on
intertwined
holding on
so tight
getting in the way of new growth
overtaking those who are not vigilant

Be vigilant!
Wack those weeds!
Make room for the new!
Make the routine!

Gloria S. Chan

Prepare
Prepare!

Waiting for those precious seeds He plants in my mind

all I can do to prepare
loosen

Breathe...

make myself loose as the soil
supple

and wait
be still enough
quiet my mind just enough

to let my courage overpower my fear
to let my faith overtake the worry
prepare prepare

until all there is left is the light
and trust
and nourishment
and protection
and more vigilance
and discipline
disciple
opening up learning new methods to
protect my crop
to call upon the rain

How ready are you to do the work it takes

Colorful Leadership

to reap the fruits of the season?

The work is done
The body rested
The faith is powerful
Our prayers answered
Everywhere we look

We reap what we sow
So what did you sow?

Everywhere I look, it's harvest time!

It's time to enjoy this special time.

He planted seeds in the mind
so I could plant them in this Earth

Everyone reaps what they sow
Choose wisely
and prepare your mind
No one can take that power
We all reap what we sow
Only if you believe what we sow will grow
What you believe will grow
So what did you sow?

It's time to witness the power of my faith.
As this journey unfolds
It's harvest time, it's harvest time
One of my favorite times.

-   Me/GSC *October 8, 2015*

....

ELEVEN

T. is for Transformative Leadership

We've worked on our *inspiration* and *intuition, mindset, purpose* and *passions, alignment,* and *courage.* Now it is time to talk about Transformative Leadership in I.M.P.A.C.T. Principle™ — walking the talk. Through transformational leadership we become instruments of peace.

So you've a grand vision! A grand plan. You've taken the preliminary steps to move it forward. Now, it is time to assess how well your leadership style brings your vision into reality. In what ways does your leadership style mirror your values? In what ways does it need some tweaking in order to better mirror your values?

For example, you might have a grand vision of peace, equality, justice, and human dignity, and yet you might have a contradictory leadership style that is full of aggression, annoyance, impatience, judgment, disdain, separation, and conflict.

This chapter is all about emotional intelligence, and walking the talk in leadership: how we relate and communicate with others, and how we manage and lead our teams and movements.

Understanding Emotion: The World as Our Mirror

Raised in a Cantonese family, the first and only thing I was taught to do in the public presence of adults was to address them by calling them "uncle" or "auntie." Otherwise, I was not really conditioned to use my words or express my feelings until much later.

Feelings? What are those? I don't think I have ever heard my mother or father express feelings unless it was a blowup of anger. We never learned to tend to our feelings. A big part of the work of *Colorful Leadership*™ is to create the space for our emotions, and the emotional needs of others. As leaders, we have the responsibility to learn about our emotions, manage them and even leverage them for growth, especially if we were not given the tools to do so in our youth.

In this chapter, we'll learn first about our own emotional triggers, and examine how to handle micro-aggressions in particular. After understanding and transforming our own emotions, we will then discuss how to communicate and negotiate with others using our emotional intelligence. In this way, we are responsive to others and at the same time care for ourselves.

What happens if we don't do this work? Lack of emotional intelligence and ineffective communication can lead to imbalanced relationships. This imbalance sometimes manifests as grudges, resentments, and blow-ups. The results are unhappy families, workplaces, and communities. Relationships can be irreparably damaged or simply dissolve.

Becoming Aware of Our Triggers

Let's start learning about our emotional landscape through our triggers. Triggers are the best and easiest way to become aware of our emotions. There reason being that our triggers are easy to identify.

What is a trigger? You know it when you feel it. You are going about your normal day, and something comes into your experience that knocks you quickly into your flight or fight stress response. You might get angry or hot. Your heart might race. You might get self-righteous! You may experience anxiety or jitters or nervousness. You may ruminate with fear about what will happen next. You might get upset or feel otherwise emotional. You might feel tired or sluggish. You might have difficulty sleeping.

When we are experiencing an emotional trigger, there is a need that is not being met. Some common triggers include when our needs are not met in the areas of security, acceptance, respect, love, appreciation, being liked, having a sense of belonging, feeling important, being right, or feeling in control.

Here are some step-by-step instructions on navigating your emotional landscape when you are experiencing an emotional trigger.

1) <u>What Triggered Your Emotional Reactivity?</u>
What happened? What about it caused so much emotion? What from your personal life and experiences are you drawing up to feel this way? When in the past have you felt this way before? Take the time to process what happened.

2) <u>What emotion did you feel? What was your stress response?</u>
Did you get angry? Frustrated? Sad? Annoyed? Combative? Did you get needy? Did you shut down? Did you engage in avoidance by burying yourself in your work or alcohol or other behaviors?

Acknowledge your feelings. It's okay to feel how you are feeling! It is a normal human reaction to the situation at hand. Your point of view and interpretation of the situation are based on your life experiences. It's as simple as that. Your feelings are valid. ALL feelings are valid feelings.

Take deep breaths to care for yourself and process your emotions. It is okay to admit to yourself that you feel hurt.

3) <u>If there were a lesson in the trigger, what would it be? What is the message?</u>

If the Universe tailor-made this emotional experience just to mold you and shape you, what would that lesson be? Thinking of the moment in this broader perspective helps to de-personalize one that feels so close to our hearts. It helps us learn from the experience. When we learn from the experience, we are able to either prevent the negative emotion from continuing or encourage the positive one to repeat and continue.

Journaling is a helpful tool to study your own emotional landscape without judgment.

EXERCISE: Keep an emotional trigger journal to better understand yourself.

What triggered your emotional reactivity?

What emotion did you feel? What was your stress response?

What is the lesson in the experience?

After a while, you will start to see patterns.

Micro-Aggressions as Tools for Empowerment

Let's look at an example. One of my clients is an Asian American woman who handles Asian American and Pacific Islander issues for a national organization. She served as an internal resource and also handled external community engagement. For one of her projects, she had to plan and facilitate a meeting on these issues. Like many women and people of color working in mainstream organizations, she over-prepared. She wanted to make sure everyone felt included, that she gathered all stakeholder input for agenda-setting purposes, that her findings were well- researched, and she created a beautiful presentation.

After all the preparation, it was time for the meeting. As she facilitated, the conversation got sidetracked as an issue came up that was not on the agenda. Next thing she knew, an hour had passed and she had yet to touch her presentation.

Inside, she started getting livid. She thought to herself:

People are disrespecting me.
They are disrespecting my work.
They don't care about my time and effort
I am invisible.
I am insignificant.
I don't exist.
I don't matter.

These thoughts were cycling rapidly throughout her mind, until finally, she shouted with great annoyance, "Don't you guys want to hear my presentation at all?"

The behavior affected her "leadership mojo" because all of a sudden she's was viewed as the crazy Asian American lady who blew up while facilitating a meeting.

During our coaching session, we looked at her response. The response was completely normal given all of my client's life experiences as an Asian American woman. She has had to fight for her voice in many other areas of her life. Given these experiences, it's no wonder that her stress response was to feel unheard.

After validating her experience, we explored exactly what about the situation had bothered her. It is essential to pinpoint the *exact reason* behind the emotion, because only then can we learn more about our desires, and what we actually want to experience. We cannot express ourselves authentically if we do not know what is inside. We need to get crystal clear about what it is we really want.

My client and I finally hit the nail on the head. It was bothering her because she didn't feel respected as a leader. Respect and Leadership were her key drivers.

So I asked the million dollar question: if you respected yourself as a leader, how would you view the situation?

Boom. Insight.

And she told me. "If I respected myself as a leader, I would have stood in my power and said: 'It seems like an important issue came up that affects everyone. This is not on the agenda, but as the facilitator and leader, I want to make sure we have space to discuss this. How do you feel about addressing this issue right now, and then scheduling another meeting to discuss the rest of the agenda?'"

So, what we coached around was how next time, she would assert her leadership and decision-making skills in the moment and move forward as a powerful leader.

Her affirmations were:

"I am a powerful leader."
"I trust 100% the decisions I make in the moment."

This is *Colorful Leadership*™ in the works. We did not coach around other people's reactions. We did not seek to fix or change others' perceptions of Asian American women as leaders. We cannot control what others believe. That would be an impossible mission. What she can do is model what powerful Asian American female leadership can look like.

What others think of you is none of your business.
Instead on focusing on others and their beliefs, we coached around cultivating her powerful leadership, shaping her own engagement in these interactions. We let the perceptions of others remain none of her business.

In other words, we built up her own self-concept around being a powerful leader.

Insight leads to freedom. Immediately the angry thoughts of frustration dancing in her mind evaporated. Know what you want, and give it to yourself. That will transform all of your experience.

After all, isn't this the harm of micro-aggressions and systemic racism, that we internalize harmful messages from outside sources? It doesn't matter whether these messages are "real" or not. The trouble is that we are perceiving them to be real, and these messages are being reinforced in very real ways in our lives. We are experiencing them as real.

The most important thing is how learn to see micro-aggressions as we see any other challenge and thus, realize the opportunity for learning and expression of our true selves in the moment. This is the work of *Colorful Leadership*™.

Be the creator of the vision that you have for the world. Create the conditions within yourself that will allow you to be the change you wish to see in the world.

We can live in despair or anger from aggressions and micro-aggressions made toward us. We can live anger and be anger. That anger may drive some of our work in the short-term, but in the long-term, it is unsustainable emotionally, spiritually, and physically. That anger has long-term effects on all aspects of our health and well-being.

What we think about becomes what we experience. If you want peace, be peace. If you want respect, embody respect. Transform yourself, and your world will transform. Don't give your power away getting stuck in an endless, torturous merry-go-around of anger, defensiveness, and self-righteousness, where there will never ever be an end to the things that consume you.

Stop giving away your power and start doing the work of transforming yourself, and through you, our world.

We can stay mad, or we can find greater freedom and power by transforming ourselves. When we choose the latter, we become the change we wish to see in the world.

They Can't Read Your Mind.

After processing your emotions, it may be appropriate to share your experiences with the people involved. Follow your intuition. Not every person needs to know everything about your emotional landscape.

When you are called to share, this work can take courage.

So often we get upset at others for not understanding us. We have to remember that they CAN'T read our minds. We have to open up and be vulnerable.

Gloria S. Chan

Step through your fear, and share your feelings. Use your words to express how you feel. What about your experience would you like to share? How would you like to see things change? What needs do you have that you would like to express? How would you like to see things grow and blossom? Remember to be respectful – not just to the person with whom you are speaking, but to yourself as well.

Sounds simple and scary at the same time? Don't worry. Communication is never perfect. We are humans, after all. That said, our communication muscles grow if we work them.

Every so often, I've noticed that I've been getting upset at my husband for not reading my mind. How unfair! Sometimes, I am so used to being in my own mind that I assume that everyone else is there with me, especially intimate loved ones. How brilliantly smooth our relationships would become with our business partners, co-workers, and families if we just shared our experiences of the situation, asked for what we need, and asked for what we truly want?

And so I did. I told my husband how I felt and what I wanted, and being the amazing person he is, he listened to my every word. It is not the job of our loved ones, partners, and co-workers to read our minds. They might guess, but they cannot know what we are thinking. By expressing ourselves and our needs, we bring them into our world and help them understand what we are going through.

Remember that everyone is doing their very best in the moment. Assuming positive intent from others helps us stand in a place of power when we express our needs.

Let go of the outcome.
Of course, there is much vulnerability to doing this. We aren't taught to share our feelings and experiences. It puts us in an emotionally suscepti-

172

ble position. What if they don't care? What if they can't deliver?

In order to stand centered and grounded in our own Power, we can't be attached to the outcome. When we make our happiness contingent upon a particular outcome, we give all of our power away to the choices and behavior of others. The important thing to remember is not to be attached to the outcome. Manage your own expectations and be open to any response that the Universe has in store for you. Be open. We can express our needs, and have no expectations at the same time.

It is when we are open and take the risk that the magic happens! In order to get what we truly want in our world, we have to be brave, tell the truth and ask for what we need and want. Don't forget there is power in vulnerability.

> EXERCISE: In which relationships are your needs unmet? What courageous conversations are you ready to have to express what you need? How can you share vulnerably and still remain unattached to the outcome?

Negotiations: Standing in Your Power

Now that we have worked through some of our own emotional landscape, it is time to discuss our interactions and negotiations with others.

We all negotiate every single day. Negotiations come in many forms. We negotiate when we decide which roommate or partner does the dishes, determine the terms of a new collaboration or partnership, and ask for a change in salary, job title or work responsibilities. Everybody negotiates, all the time.

Negotiating is soliciting the help, energy, and participation of others to create the life we want, and to change the world, together.

The following are tips to stand powerfully in negotiation. This entails cleaning up our negotiation mindset, as well as skills to try when we are actually in the process of negotiations.

Know your vision and values

Know your vision. What is your vision for this collaboration, partnership, and relationship? What is most important to you? What would the ideal look like for you? Why? It is so important to be crystal clear not only about what you want, but also why you want it.

When you are clear about your motivations and your values, then you can be open to creating solutions that honor those motivations and values, and the best outcome may not necessarily be exactly what you had in mind.

Are your motivations based on fear, or vision?

Are you motivations based on fear or based on a pure vision of what you desire? For example, if negotiations don't go your way, do you fear losing the approval and respect of others, or not reaching a certain status in society, or not having enough resources? The more personal work you do to remove fear and build your confidence and sense of security, the more successful you will be in interacting with others and holding space expansive enough for two or more people.

Clear the fear!

Step into authentic gratitude, appreciation, and excitement, not anxiety, anger, or entitlement.

Authentic appreciation goes a long way. Before you even step into the negotiation room, imagine filling yourself with that gratitude, appreciation and excitement. You will get better results and strengthen your relationship with the other party. By cultivating positivity within you, you will build real trust, the solid foundation for a powerful conversation. You will set yourself up to be able to listen to the vision, values and concerns of the other party with openness. Most importantly, you will be open to have a real conversation to develop a common vision and mutual purpose.

Here are some questions to help guide you. What do you love about the current partnership, relationship, or interaction? If it is a new relationship, what are you most excited about? This applies whether you are negotiating with a voter, a coalition member, a new boss, a friend, a partner. In order to express your authentic gratitude, appreciation, and excitement, you have to know what is at the root of your gratitude and excitement.

If you haven't done this introspective, authentic work, you show up with inauthentic gratitude, simply checking the box of positivity. Think about it. If you are negotiating with someone who is filled with anxiety, fear, anger, or entitlement, how willing would you be to create and implement a vision or plan with them? How much to you trust the end result? And with that skepticism, how much would you be willing to engage in honest negotiation?

Assume positive intent to effectively prevent or manage emotional reactivity.

PepsiCo CEO Indra Nooyi says the best advice she ever received was to assume positive intent. The best way to cause a breakdown in negotiations is to be emotionally reactive. When we assume that the other party is out to get us, we are stuck in the past. We are afraid that the other party will hurt us or take advantage of us like we've been hurt before. And so we fight. We let the past predict the future. When we assume positive intent, we open ourselves up to see the true perspective of the other person, and be able to really hear what they are communicating, including listening for their vision and values. Through deep listening, we become open to opportunities and futures that are brighter than what we've experienced before.

EXERCISE: For one week, I invite you to try on the practice of assuming positive intent in every single interaction you have. See what happens.

In your journal, make note of any experiences that stand out. What insights did you gain? In which relationships and interactions did you notice great willingness to assume positive intent? In which relationships and interactions did you feel greatest challenge? What were the differences between those situations?

Listen for the vision and values of the other parties.

As we negotiate with others, and in the partnership, collaboration and relationship, we need to make space for other people and their vision, not just our own vision. Listen for their vision and their values.

Too often we go into negotiations and high-stakes conversations with only our own perspective or agenda in mind. We may listen to others only to prepare our own responses in a way that supports our own conclusions.

This is not the way to listen with high emotional intelligence. We must learn to develop active listening skills, through which we listen intently to understand, with no agenda.

To develop active listening skills, try a technique called reflecting or mirroring. This simply means to repeat back what you believe the other person has tried to express to you. Let them know what you have heard them say. The purpose is to ensure you truly understand the point they are trying to convey, give them the opportunity to correct or elaborate if you didn't get the full picture, and ultimately make sure you are both on the same page. A good way to practice mirroring is to say, "So what I'm hearing you say is...." Finally, wait a moment before stating your point. Allow the conversation to breathe. Remember: the conversation is not a boxing match.

Create win-win solutions and be open to creative alternatives.
Now that we've looked at our vision, and their vision, let's talk about the common vision. What does a common vision look like? What are mutual values that you would like to honor? What you come up with *together* might be light-years more awesome than what any one of you could have come up with on your own.

Show an openness to create true win-win solutions. Let go of the need to have the end result look exactly like you envisioned it. Be flexible in the outcome, while honoring your own values and bottom line.

Here's a tip! Ask powerful open-ended questions that highlight collaboration and mutuality. Begin your questions with how or what. Some great questions: What is our common vision? What are the most important values that we would like to honor by the end of our negotiation? How can we honor all of those values? What are some solutions and alternatives that honor all parties? What are some first steps? Wait for their answers and brainstorm together.

Know your bottom line and when to step away.
Creating space for others does not mean allowing yourself to get trampled. Know your bottom line, and your own values. If the partnership, relationship, or interaction is not a good fit, follow your instincts and walk away. Being a powerful negotiator does not mean you come up with a

win-win every single time. It also entails the ability to walk away gracefully.

Networking as Inspired Tribe-building

We have talked about our personal emotional landscapes. We have also examined some concepts that are important when in negotiation with others. Now let's discuss our leadership in a community setting. In what ways do we lead by building community?

Lots of professionals that I coach and train say that they hate networking. They hate going out, collecting business cards, schmoozing to get ahead and land a job. There's something icky about it. It's inauthentic, manipulative, conniving, and competitive in a dog eat dog world. And they don't want to play the game.

Well, if THAT'S what you think of networking, then it's no wonder you feel crappy about it, and it's no wonder you're not getting out there! It all makes perfect sense.

Remember our mindset! What we think affects how we feel and how we physically react, and that in turn affects the way we behave. In other words, THOUGHTS => EMOTIONS => BEHAVIOR => RESULTS.

Take for example, the person who hates networking. Let's call him Jason. Jason's perception of networking is that it's nasty, rude, and fake. And he judges people who network, and all networking events as fake. He feels annoyance, judgment, and frustration when he thinks about networking. Due to this perception and emotional response, he avoids it all together, or when he attends events, he may stand on the sideline with a friend that he trusts and talks about how fake and annoying the people are. He doesn't meet anyone new, and finds his limited effort a waste of time. Jason's thoughts created his emotions and shaped his actions and results. Change yourself and your world changes.

I'd like to offer a new thought, or new definition of networking. What if I told you that networking is building an authentic tribe that uplifts everyone involved! Networking is not just about getting what you want and need. It's also about giving and contributing yourself. It is about being in community.

Networking is nurturing a community of amazing people with common interests that uplifts you, and to which you contribute your energy, talent, gifts and inspiration.

So let's meet Sharla, who believes this to be true. With this perception, she feels great about meeting new people. She is excited when she leaves the door, knowing that anyone she meets may be a member of her tribe. This openness shapes her behavior. It allows her to share who she really is, what she is passionate about, and her direction in life and career, even uncertainty, with authenticity. The result is that her passion and genuineness is infectious. People are excited to meet her, and are interested in hearing what she has to say. Those that resonate with her vision follow-up, and those who do not, no problem. The result is a community of people that she supports, and that support her. She connects without an ask. And when the time comes to ask, many people rise to the occasion to provide support.

This is the true power of networking. A tribe that helps connect you with your purpose and passion. A tribe that you support to do the same.

> EXERCISE: I invite you to brainstorm and free-write a list of attributes and characteristics of your tribe, and see what comes. Who is your tribe? Who are you excited to meet? What kind of community would you like to surround yourself with? What interests, values, and passions do those in your ideal tribe have in common? What purpose do you have in connecting with your tribe?

The Magic Mic

In addition to nurturing community, another aspect of walking the talk and making impact in the world is our thought leadership.

I offer you the magic mic question! This is a genius question that will get to the heart of your thought leadership for this season. The answer to this powerful question is deeply intertwined with your passion and purpose of the season.

> EXERCISE: Imagine you had a magic mic for 3 minutes. The mic has the power of sharing a single message with a specific group of people. After speaking into this mic, this audience is able to truly digest your message at a deep level. Not only do they understand, but the message will have ripple effects for this audience and beyond.
> What message do you communicate and to whom?

Connect with your intuition. Imagine you only have this mic one time every three years. What are three possible messages that you could share this time around? With which three possible audiences would you share it?

I ask for three to give you room to brainstorm. Among your answers lies your legacy and thought leadership for the season. Toward which message are you guided? Remember, we always grow and change, so we will have multiple callings in this lifetime if that is meant for us. My message this season is the message of radical, unconditional love — of self and others — for women of color who are called to be transformational, social, visionary leaders in this moment in time.

After coming up with your audience and the message, create a plan to start taking the first steps to build this voice.

Whether you are a speaker, a writer, artist, organizer, teacher, politician, or share your voice in other ways, don't keep YOU to yourself. You are meant to make a difference.

EXERCISE: Create your thought leadership plan.

What's the brilliant, important, critical message you have to share?

Who is your audience?

Brainstorm a list of ways to share your message. Where does this group of people convene? In what physical locations do they gather? Where is their digital home? What blogs are they reading? Do they love to read books? What TV or radio outlets do they love? What conferences or events do they attend? Where locally might you find them? Where do they live, work, eat, socialize, exercise, meditate, and play?

Develop a thought leadership plan. Choose three methods through which you will share your thought leadership. Set goals for yourself within certain time frames.

Your Voice and Leadership Are Not Meant for Everyone

Let's take a look at what might keeping you from moving forward. When genius leaders have something new and different to say, it may be scary to move forward. You might think: people will judge me, laugh at me, attack me, be mean to me.

Will they? Sure. Some people might judge you, laugh at you, gossip about you. Your gifts and talents are needed in the world anyway. Your story must be told. It is meant to be shared. That is how the world will be changed.

Let your fear guide you. Behind it is your treasure.

That is why courage is needed. A big part of discovering our voice is to speak our truths unconditionally and follow our gut about when to share and with whom to share it. Our voices and messages are not meant for everyone. Get your mind off the haters!

Not everyone will like you. At the bottom of our hearts, it is a very valid and normal human emotion to want to be liked. Anyone in the public eye knows that that just isn't real. You cannot control how someone resonates with who you truly are.

Everyone is coming with their own personal histories, and you just can't resonate with everyone. It's not personal. You are not meant to resonate with everyone! To be liked is not your purpose in life. The work of your life isn't about getting everyone to like you. It's not even important that everyone will understand you. The most important is to do the work of being you, so that you attract the people and resources that you are meant to attract. This will not only help you create an authentic and fulfilling life and career, this is how to live your purpose. Remember, you will inspire the people that you were meant to uniquely inspire. And this will not be everybody.

If you let your true self shine, you will attract people who share your values, who support your leadership. You can build your team, your crew, your people. This, my friends, is true community.

You are the heartbeat of your own network.

Find the people who want to connect with you, and you will build the courage to keep going. At the end of our days, everyone else's interpretation doesn't really matter. How they interpret your words is exactly how they are meant to hear them on their journey. What you dare speak powerfully is exactly what you are meant to on yours.

SPEAK WITH NO FILTER

We stand in powerful truths
and speak with our Voices unfiltered

first as a whisper
then
as unbridled powerful presence

in front of audiences we were born
to move and inspire and enlighten

This voice is not meant for everyone
Not all will agree or understand

It is not our job to be agreeable
or to please

even those we thought would understand
might not

And disappointments happen
we are human after all
living this human experience
in this human body
with these human needs
and this human heart

validate me
There is no guarantee

There's only one who can truly Validate
and truly See me

And when I stand in that pure light
oh the power that i will be

Through that One
what an exciting song and dance
to let the Voice come through
And finally hear what
I sound like
unfiltered.

- Me / GSC
2016

TWELVE

....

THE PERSONAL IS GLOBAL:
The Journey from Self 2.0 to 3.0

Congratulations! We have come a long way on this journey. The transformation from Self 1.0 to 2.0 was about moving from unconscious living, or living by default, through the Awakening to living by choice. We have awakened and have caught small glimpses of our true nature, and our true power, and we are learning how to walk authentically in our lives. We have gone through the personal and courageous transformations by following tips and exercises of the I.M.P.A.C.T. Principle™.

For those of you intently doing the work with commitment and rigor, at some point, you'll feel that you've reached a new level of self. Here's to You 3.0.

The New You has arrived.

The New You 3.0 is the next version of you that has gotten into the powerful habit of being your authentic self. It is the You that has gotten courageous and "used to" being You, authentically. It is no longer a struggle to speak in your authentic voice powerfully. The New You is continuously exploring what your calling and purpose is, and at some point, it clicks. The assignment of the season, the work that You are meant to do out in the world is here. You'll know it with ultimate clarity. And just like that, a new season will have arrived.

For me, Gloria 3.0 happened when I met Dr. Towanna Freeman. When she shared her vision of diversity and coaching, I knew that I had met my professional match. *CoachDiversity Institute*™ was born from our combined alchemy. We were the answer to each other's prayers. From that moment, we have been doing the impactful we were meant to do in the world in this moment in time.

It is a time of great, powerful activity. During this time, we apply what we have learned during our inward journey toward personal empowerment to the outward work of empowering community, society, and ultimately the world.

This is the work of our time.

THIRTEEN

....

The Power of Shadow Work

Our "shadow" is our biggest blind spot both as an individual and as a society. Our shadow is the part of us of which we are not aware. It is the unconscious aspect of our selves, and it is unconscious because our conscious self rejects and does not identify with it. It is the part of us that causes us shame. Because it is the part of ourselves that we reject, it is largely "negative" and is wholly unconscious, i.e. we are unaware of it by definition.

In order to make social impact in a conscious way, we must become aware of our shadow.

When we become conscious of aspects of our shadow, we can leverage it to be our biggest ally in creating the work of our lives.

So, what does a shadow look like in real life?

First, let's take a look at some examples in our personal lives before we get to the bigger picture of societal impact.

We've previously discussed aspects of our shadow, including our doubt, our worry, and our inner critics. If you want a new career, your unconscious self might be too scared to start anew; it may not believe that you have the credentials for the job you really want, even if you are fully qualified; this part of yourself may even be afraid of the ultimate freedom that you think you want. If you want a loving healthy relationship, your shadow (as mine did in my teens and early to mid-twenties) may actually really love the thrill of chasing and never catching, may be addicted to loneliness or wanting, and may find some romanticism in the loneliness and the human tragedy of heartache.

In other words, our shadow is that part of us of which we are unconscious that sabotages our dreams and desires.

Getting to know your shadow is a thrilling experience, and it can change your life. The willingness to explore the shadow moves aspects from the darkness of the shadow to the light of your conscious awake awareness.

What We Say We Don't Want
Now, let's explore the part of our shadow that really desires what we say we don't want. Getting to know this part of our shadow lessens self-sabotage. Our conscious self and bits of our unconscious self integrate and become One. We can make decisions from a powerful foundation when we know the entirety of what we are working with.

Here's a small example of this specific shadow work in my personal life. Over the holidays in 2015, my husband, my son and I went to visit my parents' at their home in Queens. My mother does a lot of worrying. She worries that I'll get sick or she worries that the baby will get sick. She worries about sickness in the past, the present, the future, and all potential illness. And she vocalizes this worry often through what one might call "annoying fussing." Even when I was little, she would do the same, worry that we weren't wearing enough clothes, or that we would catch a cold. And inevitably, it would be a self-fulfilling prophecy. I would start to worry, and then a cold comes. And I say to myself, *"aghhh, mom's going to be mad because I got a cold,"* or *"I'm gonna hear it: I told you so"* or even *"I'm not a good daughter if I get a cold, because I should have listened to my mother more."* What a pain it all was!

Well during this visit, by the time I was in bed, I started to feel my throat get a bit scratchy, my head aching a bit, and I was definitely on track to get a cold. I was trying to fall asleep and all these old thoughts came back. *"Here we go,"* *"I'm getting sick,"* *"I really don't want to get sick,"* *"Mom is going to be right again,"* and even some blaming: *"Her annoying brainwashing is making me sick,"* and *"it's her fault."*

All of this was conscious thinking. Then, I started digging deeper into my shadow. In my half-sleep state, I started wondering, what part of me actually wants to get sick? What is the subtler shadow aspect of me that wants my mom to have this "victory" and to be "right"? That was an easy answer. There is a part of me that wants to blame her, that wants to keep her villainous. With a villain, I would have more to grow, more to learn, more to share with all of you reading here. I would be able to stick with my righteousness and make her wrong. To my mother: if you are reading, this is not about you, it's about me!

So what happened? Once I became aware that my shadow actually wanted me to get sick and actually wanted to keep my mother villainous, I started loosening up on the blame game, and letting go of fighting mom in my own mind, and finally fell asleep. With just that simple awareness, the next morning, the scratchiness in my throat was all gone (as I just KNEW it would be — check the power of positive expectation!), and after one day with a slight headache, I fully staved off a cold with my mind.

Making nice with your shadow will help you reach your goals.

Working with the shadow fascinates me. And that's what a lot of coaching is. Some of coaching deals with getting clarity with your conscious thoughts. And much of coaching is unveiling the subconscious aspects that you might not be aware of, and "making nice" with those aspects and letting them go.

FOURTEEN

....

Our Shadows and Systemic Change

So what does this particular shadow work have to do with dismantling the systems of injustice in our world?

If you want a change (any change at all), a powerful question to ask is the following: what part of me benefits from the status quo?

The reason this question is important is what we discussed earlier about mindset. If our individual thoughts lead to emotions that lead to behaviors that lead to results in our personal lives, then the same rationale may be applied to the collective. Collective thoughts lead to collective emotions that lead to collective behaviors that lead to results for the collective. If our collective experience is undesirable, we must look at our collective psyche to make change. If the practices that I know as a coach have amazing potential for transformation on a personal level, who am I as an agent of change not to apply them to community and society?

Think global, act local. Asking ourselves these fundamental questions will shake up the foundations of what's keeping these systems in place within each of us. If we want to end systemic injustice, we have to ask, what part of us benefits from the status quo continuing to exist? How is our collective mindset creating and recreating the status quo? How ready are we to stop looking outward for causes and culprits, and turn inward for the answers?

If each of us answers these questions, we shake up entire foundations of this system and begin to do the work of loosening its grip on our world.

Those questions are not ones that I answer often. But when I first took a look, I sure did have some answers.

What part of me benefits from racism and sexism, and the intersection of the two?

My deep, meaningful, soulful, heartfelt sisterhood with women of color is a wonderful benefit that I enjoy that has its origins in racism, sexism, and the intersection of the two. If we truly lived in a colorblind world in which people of all races, and all people along the masculine-feminine spectrum were accepted, respected, loved, and whole regardless of their genitalia, there would be no sisterhood of women of color as it exists today. It will have evolved. Humanity will have evolved. The closeness that I feel with all of you would be different and will have matured and changed, and perhaps even dissipated.

I felt this during my 1L year at Harvard Law School. I strongly identified as being a woman of color. In my class there was a multi-racial woman. I was intrigued by her free spirit, her progressive thought, and her care for community. Because I saw her as a fellow woman of color, I assumed that we would enjoy a special sisterhood. I brought this up to her one time in discussion, and said "don't you feel like we have a greater affinity because we are women of color?" She answered, "No. I don't see you as any different than a White woman."

Ouch! I remember feeling disappointed, a bit heart-broken even, and lonelier in an already alienating campus. I wasn't yet ready to let that special sisterhood go.

Today, I'm definitely more ready. And I'll tell you why. I know I still have work to do in this sisterhood. Hence, this book. But when I do this work today, I do it with non-attachment and complete openness to other perspectives that I did not have before. I do it with honor and reverence for each of you as essential members of humanity. Each of us plays a unique role in moving humanity forward. We each have a place in the evolution of our societies, even those we do not agree with.

We still have healing to do together, and we still have healing to do in our communities. Racism and sexism still exist. We still have impulses to heal in our communities that are built around social identification. Our intuitions are still pointing us to work within community. I will keep doing work in our communities up until the day that I stop receiving impulses to do so. My intuition will tell me when the work is finished.

As we mature, grow and open up, we will continue to evolve and our communities will follow suit. As I continue walking my path, my capacity to absorb, understand, and empathize with the perspectives of all people is continuing to grow. After I left politics, there was a period of about three years that I just couldn't watch the news anymore. I had to guard myself from the ideological aggressions between liberals and conservatives. I needed protection from all the negativity that I couldn't stand. I needed space to explore in peace, and to find my place in the world.

I noticed that after *CoachDiversity Institute*™ was launched, and after we held the inspiring, challenging, thought-provoking inaugural weekend, I found a new place in the world. I stood grounded and secure in my next assignment. And after that weekend, I noticed that I started to watch the news again with interest and curiosity, purpose and mission. When we do the work of finding ourselves, we start feeling at peace and at ease, no matter the situation.

Later that week, I found myself observing a radio show that featured interview with three White male executive leaders. Previously, I may have just complained in my mind about the lack of diversity. That day, I listened. I listened carefully and intently to their stories with curiosity and was intrigued by their stories. Two of them had parents who were farmers, just like my parents in China. I noticed how I was showing up so curious. On the way home from that observation, I tuned the dial to conservative radio to see how much I could lean into curiosity. I felt that a whole new world was opening up. When I got home, I shared with my husband, who is also White, how interesting it was to learn about the deep personal stories of White men.

What would it feel like if we approached each and every person we met with reverence, awe, and curiosity, no matter who they were, no matter what their views, and no matter how fundamentally we disagreed with them? What if we listened deeply to what shaped their viewpoints, and understood? What if we truly had a deep understanding that they too are playing their part in the evolution of humanity?

What if we approached each and every person we meet with the reverence with which we wished they approached us? What if we walked the talk before needing anyone else to act in any certain way toward us? What if our commitment to our vision were unconditional?

How would the world be different then?

EXERCISE: To whom are you ready and willing to listen with greater curiosity? With which types of people are you ready to engage with less judgment? What do you wish for humanity? How willing are you to walk the talk, now, unconditionally?

Who would I be without my race? What role does racism have in your life?

This also had an easy answer. Without my race or ethnicity or my racial perspective, I wouldn't be me as I know myself today. I wouldn't have the same sense of purpose that I do now. If there were no racism, my reason for being would be different. And that is difficult for my ego, my small earthly self, to swallow.

Importantly, in all of my leadership development starting in high school throughout my entire career, racism and racial identity has given me a seat at the table. The fact that I am a woman of color has given me a platform on which to speak, be heard, and feel important. I've often been the result of Asian American affirmative action at that table. It has given me the opportunity to be an executive director of a caucus and president and CEO of a national nonprofit. There is a shadow part of me that thrives off of this conditional access and fleeting power. There is a shadow part of the community that thrives off of this fleeting power. There is a shadow part of me, certainly a part of the ego, that is afraid that if racism ends, that I would no longer have a voice and be important. The "shadow" part of me is not ready to give up that platform for leading. This "shadow" part of me is unaware of my True Power, the inherent power that is in each of us.

Remember, our "shadows" are the parts of us that we deny. For this very reason, it is uncomfortable to look at the ways in which we benefit from the status quo. These inquiries and this work are not for the faint of heart.

EXERCISE: Ask yourself these questions with complete non-judgment. Who would I be without my race? What part of me benefits from the status quo? In what ways am I empowered in the current system?

FIFTEEN

....

Grieving The Race Card

The ego fears change. The ego fears a racism-free world. All that we have known are the racial structures that exist. The very foundations of our identities have been shaped by the status quo. There is a limited sense of security and belonging that comes with our racial identities. There is a deep sisterhood that comes with these identities.

However, if we are to create a world without racism, we must find a sense of security that is not based on any particular identity or condition. Rather, we have to find it within ourselves to cultivate a sense of security and belonging that is bigger than our race. To do so, we must tap into a powerful sense of belonging and safety that is inherent in the divinity of Human existence. When we acknowledge that we are part of a larger fabric, there is no need to grasp for power or grasp for identity. We become secure in our True Identity.

Here is an example. Each year is a tough year for the Black community with respect to police killings. In 2014 and 2015, the public consciousness of these deaths was raised with each case after prominent case: Eric Garner, John Crawford III, Michael Brown Jr., Dante Parker, Tamir Rice, and Sandra Bland.

Each of these had a tremendous emotional and spiritual impact on one of my clients who was head of racial justice and racial healing work in a prominent foundation.

What made her the most reactive though, was Rachel Dolezal, a White woman who passed herself as a Black activist. The sentiment was rage, and it went something like this: "how dare she appropriate my Black womanhood? This Black womanhood that it took me over three decades to integrate. This Black womanhood that I grieved and struggled with. A Black womanhood through which it took me years to find my power. How dare she?"

A part of my client knew that if her mission was to dismantle racism, then she must accept that race is a construct that has formed into a vehicle of discrimination, violence, and hate. She knew that her anger at Rachel simply strengthened that construct. At a gut level, she knew that she had to let go of her race card.

As her coach, I asked her, if the Universe tailor-made Rachel Dolezal just for her, what would that purpose be?

After a moment of conscious thought, she had it. Through Rachel and the media frenzy she caused, my client was able to put conversations about race at the forefront of her foundation, both at a domestic level and internationally. Rachel's actions led to a seemingly localized, and subsequently nationalized conversation. It was this conversation that enabled my client to superpower her racial healing and racial justice work, and bring it to the forefront at her organization. She was able to have meaningful conversations with White men and White women about race because of Rachel. Brilliant.

I then asked her: "with this new knowledge what do you want to do now?" She told me that she would stand in her powerful leadership for the rest of her time at the foundation. She was going to shake up that foundation that year. And she did.

Together, my client was able to process her emotion, let go of resentment and anger, and leverage the experience to give further power and meaning to her work.

When it's time, we get to turn in our race cards when we are ready.

Don't get me wrong. Today, there is still a need for systemic analysis around social injustices. There is still systemic suffering that impacts our communities along racial lines. There is still pain that needs to be addressed and truths acknowledged. Turning in our race cards means acknowledging the richness and pain of our racial experiences, and not letting this trauma or current racial realities define who we get to be.

Furthermore, it is still meaningful and important to celebrate our history, heritage, and culture. I don't mean that we need to let go of these aspects of our experience.

Instead, turning in our race card simply means focusing on what is possible with fervor, hope, and discipline — even in the face of despair and grief.

Turning in our race card means living our own lives without limits, even as we bump up against old limits created by old thinking. It means carrying ourselves spiritually, emotionally, and mentally with great power. In means believing in our visions of justice and equality so much that we begin to walk the talk of love and community unconditionally, and summon it into reality.

In order to live in a just world, there must be no limit to our understanding of our own power. Only then can we begin to create relationships and communities while standing in our full power. Only then can we make the impact that we were born to make — powerfully. Only then can new worlds be created. Only then can we shape our own futures. Only then can we create new communities that treat all people with respect and dignity.

Putting down our race card means no longer pointing fingers and blaming anyone else. It means letting go of blame itself. It means trusting in our personal power.

No amount of finger pointing leads to freedom. So, we let go.

We are so much more than the limited identities that we were assigned. With this new knowledge, we open our eyes and ears, speak the Truth, and help others do the same. It means testifying the Truth, reaching for our vision, all while letting go of pointing fingers.

The space that I am meant to hold is the space for women of color to start this controversial, spiritual, and mind-bending work. These are the women that I am meant to serve in this process. We all have our calling in the movement toward greater humanity. It is our choice whether we respond to this call.

Grieving this race card is not as scary as the "shadow" or the ego thinks. We can do work this courageous and brave work that will change our world, together.

Let us proceed in our powerful alchemy.

EXERCISE: What does your race card mean to you? In what ways are you ready to let go, and find greater security in your Inner Power? In what ways are you not yet ready? How can we honor our history, but not let it limit our future? What new insights are you experiencing around racial identity?

KEEP WALKING

Keep walking.
Keep following.
Keep trusting.
Keep listening for the Guide.

Stand in powerful leadership.
Speak the Truth,
no matter what.
Keep leading.
Be unafraid.
Your Family will find you.

Keep allowing.
Keep trusting.
Keep knowing that in this TRUST our world is
            constantly   evolving.
We are helping it to evolve and change.

Change is inevitable.

We can either believe it is crashing
or believe that it is growing.
Both are true.

Gloria S. Chan

What we believe is true.
Our mind and spirit and body are
more powerful than we can possibly understand.

Our questions
our precious questions

Our role as the Coach Teacher Inspirer Artist Brave Leader:
We are to ask the hard delicious questions
that reveal the most powerful beautiful ugly answers
that will propel us into the future
forward into human progress
Into a world where we know
the power of unconditional love
of self, of other, of all.

It is inevitable
as we follow our guided impulses and deep inner wisdom.

We know the Truth about one another.

We are each other's home.

We are each other's peace.

We are each other's shadows.

The world that we dream of is not only possible
it will arrive sooner than we think

Our shadows are made whole
transformed into light.

Colorful Leadership

As we walk with courage
more shadows will undoubtedly appear, as
we courageously keep seeking.

We walk the talk in the world.
And so, our dream will arrive sooner than we think.

- Me/GSC
  2016

SIXTEEN

....

A Lifetime Worthy of YOU

While this chapter of our journey together is coming to a close, our work has just begun.

This book has been focused on expanding your awareness of who it is that you really are, and how discovering the fullness of our power will help us bring our visions into reality. Together, we will transform our world.

I love the Albert Einstein quote:

"We cannot solve our problems with the same thinking we used when we created them."

It is so important to do the work to change our thinking, our feeling, and our being.

More important than motivation or inspiration, I hope that you have committed to doing the work it takes to create a life and career that you love. I hope that you have been inspired, and have access to all the tools you need to live life in Full Color.

In my late twenties, a friend noted in a pejorative way that I have live a charmed life. I took that with a hint of guilt that my friend meant that I lived a life without struggle. I took it as an accusation that I was not a victim in the same way that she was.

Today, I acknowledge that I live a fully charmed life. I revel in it. It is an amazing, magical, synchronistic life full of surprises, delight, and hardship too. That hardship is so easy to embrace because I know now that it all has a greater purpose and it will point me to the next greater version myself.

Ever since the Awakening, I have grown to fuller, deeper, and wiser versions of myself. My work gets easier, faster, and more delightful. When new challenges come my way, I know that I can handle it. My commitment is to my growth, even when growth is painful.

I know that if you do the work of the I.M.P.A.C.T. Principle™, you will start living a charmed life too, and start living the impactful life of your dreams.

You too are powerful, ever-expanding, and ever-growing. You too are deeply connected to Infinite Wisdom. You are unconditional love. You have a *firestorm* in you. You are bold and unlimited. Stay steady in the work of connecting with your Power. I look forward to meeting that next more powerful version of YOU.

We are salt of the earth. We all have overcome amazing obstacles, and have the passion and drive to change in the world. Let's leverage this power and make our ultimate transformations.

Here's to our lives' work, together.

Here's to our powerful alchemy that we continually refine.

Here's to living life in Full Color.

Here's to a lifetime that is worthy of you.

USING THIS BOOK AS A STUDY GUIDE

....

For Individuals and Small Groups

I hope you enjoyed this book, and that you received what you needed as you read it. I hope for deep shifts and sustainable change in your life. You have everything you need to live life in Full Color.

Remember, it is not enough to have insights. Real change happens when you apply your insights and learning and put it to practice. Real change happens when we do something differently.

Keep a journal with you on this journey. Apply your insights in your life, reflect upon those applications, and reach even deeper insight. Expand!

To add even greater momentum and power to your work, share this resources and your journey with others. Choose a trusted study partner or small group. When we share vulnerably, we push each other to deeper understanding in a safe space. Listen to one another, respect one another, and hold the space for deep learning. Go chapter by chapter. Do each exercise together. Dig deeper.

Use this book as a study guide for yourself, your work in pairs, and group discussions.

I welcome you to contact me at any time with any questions and challenges that you come across either in your own work or your work with others. You may reach me at info@gloriaschan.com.

Also feel free to contact me to share your success and celebrations!

I would love to hear from you.

SEEKING GUIDANCE?

....

Congratulations on doing the inner work! This work takes courage and consistency. Are you wanting personalized support on your journey? Learn about Gloria's coaching services at www.gloriaschan.com or email info@gloriaschan.com.

What others are saying

"Gloria believes in me even stronger than I do and even when she's not next to me, I am pushed to see the awesome in me because I hear her voice in my head."
- Allison Brown, Executive Director, Communities for Just Schools Fund

"I feel like I have complete control over my destiny and that I have the power to create the life that I want. That feeling is what has made every dollar and every minute working with Gloria worth it."
- Lillie Madali, Deputy Director, City of Atlanta

"Gloria's core strength is her ability to see the big picture and to break it down into tangible and actionable steps."
- Grace Hwang Lynch, Writer, Editor, Communications Consultant

"Gloria has provided me with a level of thought processing that has transformed me on a personal and professional level... truly life-changing!"
- Christy Brown, Founder and CEO, Divine Endowments, Inc.

STAY CONNECTED!

....

SIGN-UP for Gloria's newsletter at www.gloriaschan.com.

FOLLOW Gloria on twitter: @gloriaschan.

LIKE Gloria on Facebook at www.facebook.com/gloriaschancoaching.

CONNECT with Gloria on LinkedIn at www.linkedin.com/in/gloriaschan.

CONTACT Gloria at info@gloriaschan.com.

ABOUT THE AUTHOR

....

Gloria S. Chan is a High I.M.P.A.C.T.™ Leadership Consultant and Senior Vice President at CoachDiversity Institute. Gloria partners with women of color, social visionaries, and their teams to skyrocket their leadership impact through speaking, facilitation, and coaching services. Her clients include senior leaders and organizations in education, nonprofit, government, corporate, foundation, journalism, and youth sectors. She is certified by the International Coach Federation as a Professional Certified Coach (PCC).

Previously, Gloria spent seven years in Asian American and Pacific Islander national advocacy in Washington, DC. She served as President and CEO of the Asian Pacific American Institute for Congressional Studies, which develops the political leadership pipeline for the Asian American and Pacific Islander community. Gloria also served in the U.S. Congress as executive director of the Congressional Asian Pacific American Caucus (CAPAC) and as legislative counsel to U.S. Rep. Michael Honda.

In 1999, she founded Chinatown Youth Initiatives (CYI), a youth leadership nonprofit for high school students in New York City. Its mission is to empower New York City youth with the knowledge and skills necessary to address the needs of Chinatown, Asian Americans, and other underrepresented communities.

Gloria received her law degree from Harvard Law School, and undergraduate degree from Swarthmore College. She is also certified as a kundalini yoga teacher through the Lighthouse Yoga Center in Washington, DC.

30589297R00137

Made in the USA
Middletown, DE
31 March 2016